THE SECRET TO A GREAT EVANGELISM MINISTRY

BibleLeague

CHICAGO, ILLINOIS

The Secret to a Great
Evangelism Ministry

STEVEN ELZINGA

The Secret to a Great Evangelism Ministry
By Steven Elzinga
Copyright ©2003 by the Bible League

Unless otherwise noted, all Scripture quotations are from the Holy Bible,
New International Version, ©1973, 1978, 1984 International Bible Society.
Used by permission of Zondervan Bible Publishers. All rights reserved.
Verses marked KJV are from the Holy Bible, King James Version.

ISBN 1-882536-64-9

Printed in the United States of America, 2003

ACKNOWLEDGEMENTS

This is the third book in a five-book series that Steve Lansingh and I have teamed up to produce. I think it is our best effort so far. Thanks, Steve.

I would also like to give a special thanks to all the people of Hope Community Church in Surrey, British Columbia—my first church plant. Much of what I learned about evangelism I learned from you.

Next, I want to send a thank-you to a Mexican-immigrant mother who endured my pre-packaged attempt to evangelize her back in 1975. God used you to show me that evangelism is more about connection than presentation.

Also, I would like to thank the Bible League—the organization I work for—an organization that, in just the last year alone, inspired ordinary believers all over the world to help more than two million people complete a Bible study for the first time. That's evangelism!

Finally I want to thank God Himself, who did not send a tract, video, or PowerPoint presentation to communicate His love for us but instead sent His own Son—Jesus—who did not just drop by for a week-long crusade but became one of us, walked with us, cried with us, died for us.

CONTENTS

PREFACE

MY BROTHER IS A FISHERMAN. I AM NOT. WELL, I AM not much of one. Every year or so I wonder if I'm missing out on something great in life, and I try fishing again. So far I have not gotten hooked. My four boys are not fishermen, either. Periodically, I feel I should try to get them hooked, but they always wriggle off any fishing plans.

My brother has one son. Both he and his son love fishing. That's the two of them on the cover. The skills and knowledge of fishing have been passed down from father to son, but it is not the skill and knowledge of fishing that makes my nephew a fisherman—it is my brother's love of fishing.

That is what this book is about: passing on the love of fishing.

As Jesus walked beside the Sea of Galilee, he saw Simon and his brother Andrew casting a net into the lake, for they were fishermen. "Come, follow me," Jesus said, "and I will make you fishers of men." At once they left their nets and followed him. — Mark 1:16-18

Steak & Chips, Hold the Peace and Love

BY NIGEL BARRETT

Fellow Londoners, I'd like to petition your help in pushing forward a new restaurant policy. Similar to the practice of offering separate seating for smokers and non-smokers, I propose additional seating that would allow me to eat in a special "non-Christian" section.

It seems that no matter where I go lately, there's a table of a dozen Christians chatting about God and praying together. They have that right, but I also have a right to eat my meal in quiet. In short, I call for a separation of church and steak.

It's not just the restaurants that are the problem. Taking a walk through Leicester Square used to be a high point of my afternoon, but now I can't make it from one side to the other without hearing a cluster of people singing something about peace and love. Personally, I'd love to just be left in peace.

At first I thought I was being paranoid, but an informal poll of our office has confirmed my suspicions: People have seen Christian groups — large and small — gathered at hotels, stadiums, homes, parks, and campuses. Whatever happened to the old days when they just stayed tucked away in their churches?

Let me be clear: I am not against any individuals practising their religion. Whatever people want to believe is fine with me. But where can I go to be among my own kind, the unbelievers? We do not have temples devoted to unbelief. The public sector, the marketplace, is all the temple we have. I just want it to be left that way. Or I will have to start getting a lot of my food for take-away.

1

THE RELUCTANT REPORTER

JACK McCLELLAN PRIDED HIMSELF ON HIS INTUITION. He could smell a good story where others could find only mundane facts. It's how he'd made his reputation as an investigative journalist. But as he handed the clipping back to his editor, he had to shrug his shoulders. "I'm not sure I get it," he said. "What's the story?"

"To be honest, I'm glad you don't see it," said Lucas Hudson, smiling. "That means it's likely no one else has taken notice, and we could break an exclusive."

Hudson got out of his chair and walked over to the floor-to-ceiling windows. The offices of *The Global Journal* were on the thirtieth floor of the Claremont Building, over-looking much of New York City. With the sun low in the sky, his squat body transformed into a striking silhouette.

"You ever go to church, Jack?"

Jack hesitated. It seemed like a rather personal question for a business meeting. "When I was young," he answered vaguely. Hudson didn't really need to hear how he'd lost his taste for Mass after his parents divorced.

"Good," Hudson said. "Well, not good exactly, but you're just the reporter I need for this story: someone willing to look at the situation with an objective eye."

Jack would have called his eye untrained rather than objective, but he held his tongue to see where Hudson was going with this lead.

"See, I do go to church. I've been to church every Sunday for the past forty years, and the truth is that church in America has stagnated. Sure, there are new books, new programs, and new approaches every year — but no growth. Many church-growth experts would have us believe that the church may rebound if we can just find the right tool, the right campaign, but history doesn't support that."

Hudson walked back toward his desk, picked up a book, and tossed it at Jack. It was titled *The Rise and Fall of Christianity*, and this particular copy looked well-read.

"History tells us the American church is on the path to extinction. If you read that book, you'll find out that wherever Christianity has traveled on the globe, it spread like wildfire, then crystallized, stagnated, withered, and died."

"A pretty grim picture," Jack said, trying to imagine his reaction if, say, pro sports were being phased out.

"But I think I've spotted a reverse in the trend," Hudson said. "I keep finding these small signs of rejuvenation over in Europe, which has been stagnant even longer than America. I've collected dozens of offhand references to Christians meeting together in public places and private houses, in large groups and small, both planned and spontaneous. Most of my clippings are from England, but I've collected them from France, Belgium, and Holland, too. I'd like you to investigate further and see what's behind these reports, and what's driving this new movement."

Jack sighed. "If you're looking for someone to bring back the key to saving the church, I'm not interested."

Hudson just smiled. "That's exactly why I want you on the job. If I took the story, I'd trip over my own feet in my rush to believe everything. You can stay objective. I want to know if it actually works — if it's just another gimmick or if it's the real deal."

Jack gave his editor a wry smile. "This isn't news, you know. It's tabloid paranormal research."

Hudson didn't laugh. "This is a real story waiting to be broken, Jack. I'm talking about an undetected religious revival in Europe that could change the way churches act across the world. The political and social implications alone will make our readership drool. You'll get a cover story and thirty pages of space. I see at least a month of steady work here — not just on what's happened, but on how it happened, where it's going, human-interest angles, the works."

Jack was torn: A steady workload sounded attractive, and the national exposure would help his career. But it also seemed far too long to be stuck with a dead-end subject. Besides, it was the wrong time for him to be traveling.

"Can I think it over?" he asked.

"Look, if you don't want it, there's a dozen other —"

"It's just that it's a big commitment," Jack interrupted. "I want to talk it over with the family."

"Oh, are you married?" Hudson asked, his voice apologetic. "I was under the impression —"

"I'm divorced," Jack said uncomfortably. "Two kids.

I'm supposed to fly them out here for spring break, actually — which is only three weeks from now."

"I see," Hudson said. "Well, you might be able to crack it in three weeks if you're diligent. Think about it and let me know first thing tomorrow."

"I know I made a promise, buddy, but it'll be fun at Grannie and Grampy's place, too. You'll see."

Jack was trying to console his four-year-old, who was in despair over the likelihood of spending a week with Jack's parents. "Tell you what: I'll bring you back something special from England — anything you like."

Scott sniffed back his tears. "Really?"

"Just name it," Jack agreed quickly.

There was silence on the other end of the line as Scott thought hard. Jack began to worry he'd made another rash promise. "Something green," Scott said at last.

Jack stifled a laugh. "You got it, buddy. Any particular shade you'd like — forest green, or a lime green?"

"Green green," came the firm reply.

Jack nearly laughed again. "OK, I'll do my best. Now find Mommy and put her back on before you go to bed."

Jack heard Scott's footsteps trailing away; the bustle of a full house made his heart ache. He looked around his apartment, not much bigger than a hotel room, and thought how lifeless it all looked. Other than a few framed photos of Scott and Bethy, it was about as generic as a hotel room.

"Are you still there?" he heard his ex-wife say.

"No, I've hung up, Veronica."

"Look, I've been thinking," she continued, ignoring his sarcasm. "Spring break or no spring break, you should stick with the assignment. The kids will be disappointed, but it could mean a big raise in your profile and in your paycheck. I think it would help everyone involved if you had a steadier income — the kids seem to need new shoes every few weeks, and I know they love macaroni and cheese, but they shouldn't have to live on it."

"I know, I know," Jack said. "It's the only real choice. I just don't want the kids to feel I've abandoned them."

"Do you think they don't already feel that way?" she asked.

"One weekend a month is all I can afford to fly out, and you know that," he snapped, falling into the familiar routine of argument.

"Well, if you lived out here," Veronica countered, "we could really put that plane-fare money to better use. The purse strings might not have to be so tight."

"Are you suggesting that our kids need *stuff* more than they need their own ..." Jack let his voice trail off. He sighed. "Look, I'm sorry. You're right; I should take the assignment. It makes the most sense in the long run."

"Thank you," Veronica said.

He said his goodbyes, then flopped back on the bed and stared at the ceiling. He hadn't liked the sound of the assignment from the beginning, but he'd been bullied into it. Weeks and weeks of talking to Christians every day. Weeks of people asking him about his "eternal soul" and its "destiny," trying to win him over with zealous persuasion. He was going to have to remember to pack aspirin.

The Rise + Fall of Christianity

AVIATOR AIRLINES

"You are born. You live and flourish on the earth - then, suddenly as you came, you are gone. What is it all about? That is what religion seeks to know. ... Religion is the system men put together to make sense not only of their lives, but of life itself."

{But can a system, however well-developed, ever last?}

Chapter 1: A Ripple in the Water

"Did Jesus of Nazareth really intend to change the world? He was, after all, just a blue-collar worker from a backwater town. He took none of the usual steps on the path toward influence."

- never planted a church
- never founded a school
- no evidence He wrote anything down: no books or treatises
- never organized any groups
- never developed curriculum
- never held a seminar or retreat

He simply lived. Helped people get connected to God ... gave them a new way to relate to God {as a father}. "Life is about God's desire to bring His children back home."

**With this message, Jesus turned the Jewish practice of religion <u>for God</u> into a relationship <u>with God</u>.

AVIATOR AIRLINES

"Somehow, getting people closer to God brought people closer to each other, and He began to attract a following. He could have accomplished many things with these people" {revolt against the occupying Romans, power and riches for Himself} but instead "seemed more interested in making sure that just twelve of His followers, those who lived with Him every day, became disciples of His message."

　　*Very <u>iffy</u> plan for passing on His ideas!

Chapter 2: The Ripple Expands

"So how did Christianity survive, let alone explode onto the scene like it did? In part, Jesus' counter-intuitive model of making disciples ensured that His people didn't just talk <u>about</u> the love of God. His disciples made sure the next person understood that love well enough to be able to talk about it with someone else."

Grassroots movement kind of thing:
- no mission agencies
- no Bible schools
- no "four spiritual laws"
- no church camps

- no church buildings
- no Christian bookstores
- no Christian radio

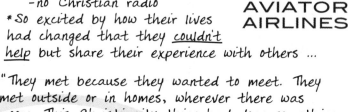
AVIATOR
AIRLINES

*So excited by how their lives had changed that they <u>couldn't help</u> but share their experience with others ...

"They met because they wanted to meet. They met outside or in homes, wherever there was room. This Christianity thing had done something to change them, given them hope and purpose in place of fear and strict duty, and they were overflowing with enthusiasm."

Chapter 3: The Ripple Becomes a Wave

"The followers of Jesus didn't stay contained in the city of Jerusalem, or even in the province of Judah. 400 years earlier the Jewish people had been scattered around the world, and word was quick to travel to each displaced Jewish community throughout the Middle East and parts of Europe."

Chapter 4: The Wave Picks up Speed

"The word got out. The message proved equally popular to those without the thousands of years of Jewish heritage that Jesus was building on. It tapped into a basic human need."

* Spread first among the commoners, the most lowly in European countries
* Thought to be a threat to the Roman Empire; Christians became persecuted; only encouraged more converts

AVIATOR AIRLINES

Chapter 5: The Wave Crashes

"For the first 300 years, authentic success was the driving force behind the Christian movement. But underground success rarely goes unnoticed - or unexploited - by those with power. Opportunists are always willing to co-opt the power of any successful movement."

* 312 A.D., Emperor Constantine sees a cross in the sky ... paints this sign on the shields of his army ... wins the battle ... converts to Christianity. He moves Christianity from a <u>persecuted</u> to a <u>preferred</u> religion throughout the empire.
* With preferred status comes money, power, buildings, bureaucracy, confusion between church and government
* Christianity moves from the home to the church building, from a grassroots movement to a political system, from a reliance on the ordinary person's testimony of a changed life to dependence on programs and a professional clergy.

Chapter 6: The Cycle Continues

AVIATOR
AIRLINES

"Christianity spreads throughout
Europe - partly through the
efforts of those who genuinely
have a burning desire to share
their relationships with God. But much of the
growth is politically or economically inspired."

- attempts to develop grassroots Christianity,
  based on genuine <u>transformation of a culture</u>
  (St. Patrick's efforts among the Celts) were
  eventually brought under the banner of the
  governmental church
- pattern continues for hundreds of years: new
  areas are reached and then brought into the
  fold, where they grow static
- the church remains largely a political, social,
  and economic institution

Chapter 7: Waves Across the Atlantic

"The discovery of the New World was seen as an
opportunity to at last break the stranglehold of
the institutional church. Persecuted groups like
the Quakers and Puritans settled in the
Americas, and the U.S. Constitution made no
provision for an official state religion."

  *But the church never recovers from the
   "preferred status" of Constantine, with its
   emphasis on money, building, clergy, and

programs. This emphasis is carried over into the New World. Despite a fresh start, sharing the gospel remains an attempt to usher people into the church institution.

AVIATOR
AIRLINES

Chapter 8: Waves of the Future

"At the beginning of the 21st century, the largest growth of Christians is concentrated in Asia + Africa. Perhaps some of this growth is driven by the genuine sharing of a relationship with God. But history has also shown: Poor people are often eager to buy what the rich foreigner is selling."

*Christianity's track record so far indicates that this movement, too, will die.
   1) Middle East: virtually no remnant of Christianity there today
   2) Europe: now Christian in name only; very nominal in practice
   3) North America: church growth is stagnant
   4) Asia and Africa: currently growing, but what do they have to look forward to?

Chapter 9: When the Last Wave Crashes

"The evidence shows that Christianity travels in waves. It begins with intense enthusiasm and transformation, settles into an institutional status quo, and then withers slowly away. ...

The only question is why.
Christians would tell you that
God moves mysteriously, and no
one knows where the Spirit
blows. Perhaps this is so.

AVIATOR AIRLINES

"But fads come in waves, too. Out of nowhere
they coalesce, spreading by word of mouth until
everyone is jumping in, hoping to feel a sense of
community. But the excitement of getting on
board {being converted} or of getting others on
board {evangelism} isn't enough to sustain the
lack of substance. The next fad, the next new
thing, takes its place.

"Does anything set Christianity apart from a
fad? In the end, no. The growing edge of
Christianity is made up of those new to the
faith and those few with a selling personality.
Where are the old Christians? Where are the old
converts? They are too bored to share their
faith. Could it be that just being a Christian,
day-in and day-out, is <u>not that exciting</u>?

"For this reason, I believe the fall of
Christianity to be imminent. Once its practices
begin to calcify in Asia and Africa, it will have
nowhere new to move where it hasn't already
left ruins. Resurgence among the debris of its
past is an improbable feat. The last wave will
crash upon the shore, and no more will follow."

2

SHORTCOMINGS OF THE SALES PITCH

"SIR?" THE FLIGHT ATTENDANT SAID, JOSTLING JACK OUT of his reading. "Would you like to have the chicken salad or the grilled fish this evening?"

"The fish," he answered by reflex.

"And you, sir?" she asked the man next to him.

"I think I'll have the same as my neighbor here."

Jack glanced at the man, wondering if perhaps he'd failed to recognize an old friend, but didn't find the wide smile or the thin nose to be familiar.

"Say, what interested you in that book?" the man asked, taking the glance to be an invitation to converse.

"Research," Jack said, and turned back to reading.

"Then you should know that the author's view is a widely contested one," his seatmate continued.

"I would imagine so," Jack said indifferently. "There are probably a lot of people who wouldn't like the idea of Christianity drying up."

His neighbor pressed on. "And I presume you're not one of them?" he asked.

Jack set down his book and turned to hold the man's gaze. "The truth is, Mr. —"

"Call me Leonard."

"Well, Leonard, the truth is that I don't much care what the future of Christianity is. It's not important to me one way or the other."

"And what about your own future?" Leonard volleyed back. "If you were to die right now, do you know where your soul would go?"

Jack smiled slightly, warming up to the idea of this chat. After all, once he was on the job in London, he wouldn't have the option of rebutting anyone who targeted him like this. "I don't believe in the soul," he said simply.

"So what do you believe in?"

Jack took a moment to gather the right words. "I'm a reporter, Leonard. I'm trained to look at things with an objective eye. The 'soul,' I've found, is a convenient way of saying that the world revolves around myself. To speak of the soul is to say that my big concern in life is what happens to me, to my 'being.' Instead, I believe what's important is the human race as a whole, that we train each generation to improve on what we've done, and eventually we human beings will find peace and harmony as a species."

"So then you ignore the problem of evil?" Leonard asked.

"No — like I said, I'm a reporter. I've seen human beings at their worst, and I have to admit that evil stands just as good a chance as peace of winning out in the end. I would just call evil 'selfishness,' and call peace 'selflessness,' and leave it at that."

Leonard smiled broadly. "Then there may be hope for you. Jesus Christ preached about selflessness all the time."

"Of course," Jack agreed, even though he couldn't remember much of Jesus' teachings offhand. "That's what made Him great. But His followers have said: 'Believe ... and you will save your soul. Believe ... and you will have spiritual power and heavenly wealth — and probably some of the earthly kind as well. Believe ... and you will find friendship and comfort and healing.' At every turn, it's all about me!"

Jack paused to let the words sink in. He continued more quietly: "I'd rather belong to a religion where membership means you comfort and heal other people, where you serve your community and your world rather than yourself."

"But," Leonard said, his brow furrowed, "that's exactly what Jesus preached. Perhaps you're focusing too much on the messengers, who are only human, and not enough on the Message."

Jack gave a skeptical look. "So it's my fault that your message is unclear? It doesn't have anything to do with how you share it with people?"

"Well, I suppose there's always room for improvement," Leonard allowed.

"No, not just room for improvement," Jack argued, feeling himself grow more heated. "Evangelizing is fundamentally flawed because you're trying to push your idea on other people. In the area of religion, where it's a very personal choice, I think we should just let people figure it out for themselves."

The flight attendant rolled the dinner cart up to their row, and the two men lowered their trays and took their dinners. Jack took a forkful of his halibut filet before he noticed Leonard praying. He felt slightly uncomfortable as he chewed the bite.

"So what you're saying," Leonard continued as soon as he stopped praying, "is that you want an unbiased guide to all belief systems without any push in a certain direction? But why should religion be different from everything else? When you think about it, most of life is spent trying to convince other people — what to buy, what to wear, where to go to school, which person to marry, what to do for a living. Why is it OK for people to push ideas in those arenas, but not in religion?"

"For starters," Jack said, "most people don't present jobs or colleges or spouses as 'the best one.' Those decisions require finding something that fits you as a person, rather than determining that one path is the only path, as religion says. Clothes and cars and junk food are another matter," he said, holding up his diet cola. "Their advertisements usually do position them as the best choice. But I don't mind it so much with products because they are just trying to sell me a 'thing' and not a view on life."

Leonard gestured pointedly with his fork. "I would disagree," he said. "I think that maybe these non-important things keep us so busy and preoccupied that we never really get around to considering the important stuff. Or worse — perhaps in a subtle way the little things get sold as big things! I mean, so many commercials promise friendship and happiness and fulfillment from carbonated water!"

"Fine," Jack said. He swallowed a mouthful of fish. "But just because companies use an ideal to sell their products, that's no reason that religions should sell their ideals as a product! Maybe that's what really gets me: that most evangelists sell their stuff as if it were no more than a hamburger. Why rely on the same marketing techniques to sell a way of life that marketers use to sell fries?"

Leonard looked perplexed. "Because it works, that's why. Marketing is marketing — you can use it to sell a million hamburgers or save a million souls. It's effective regardless of your goals."

"But just a minute ago you complained that advertisers over-hype their products," Jack said. "Advertising is *famous* for promising more than it delivers. It's a hustle, a bait-and-switch. Is that really the sort of thing you want associated with your religion?"

"But Christianity delivers what it claims. No false promises."

"Then you shouldn't need marketing at all. Let me put it this way: If the big burger joints suddenly stopped advertising tomorrow, do you think their sales would hold steady? Most people in America already have a franchise or two nearby — wouldn't they just continue with their eating habits? No. Because the product they sell isn't that good. Hamburgers have not changed people's lives." Jack absentmindedly buttered his roll. "If religion is any different — if it does transform people — then it should be like one of those movies that is a word-of-mouth hit — you know, one that plays for months and months and increases its attendance each week, because people just have to tell their friends how moving it was. If Christianity is what it says, all these changed lives should be advertising enough."

"I see what you're saying," Leonard said, chewing his food thoughtfully. "I've got a few pamphlets in the over-head bin you might want to take a look at: stories of people whose lives were changed by Jesus."

Jack rolled his eyes. "I'm not impressed by a few Christians out of millions who have really cool stories. I'd be more impressed with small stories of change in a vast number of people. Let's say that among Christians, there was only a five percent divorce rate: That would impress me. But instead, divorce among Christians is about the same as the national average, about thirty-five percent. I might be impressed if Christians were more organized, more creative, more healthy, or more reliable than any other group in America, but I just don't see it."

"Christians aren't perfect," Leonard said softly, "just forgiven. Learning to love God is a lifelong process with a lot of stumbling blocks."

Jack thought for a moment. "I'm glad to hear you say that. That sounds more like real life. But I'd still like to see that process. I'd like to witness the two steps forward and the one step back — that's the only way I'm really going to understand it. Handing me a story of grand transformation from some famous person doesn't give me any idea of what the day-to-day is like. Advertising just isn't as con-vincing as a person willing to be honest with me about the journey, on a regular basis, over the years."

Leonard smiled. "This flight is only eight hours, you know."

"I know that. And you knew that when you started this conversation. You knew you'll never see me again, but what's to lose in planting a seed, right?"

"I guess," Leonard said, shrugging.

"That's the game plan then: Drop seeds wherever you go," Jack said dryly. "Leave tracts, use bumper stickers, hold a crusade, go door-to-door, sing a Christmas carol, stick a Bible in every hotel room. I've been around long enough to know the gimmicks. But if the Christian life is really as amazing as you say — if praying to God, reading your Bible, and singing about Jesus really does something for you — then why don't I ever hear about that? Why is it always some event, some program, or some piece of paper you're touting instead of a day-in, day-out life with God?"

Leonard fumbled for an answer. "Well, no one ... I mean, if you ..."

"Because the Christian life on its own is tiresome," Jack said, cutting him off. "You need to jazz it up, to get other people excited, in order to make it exciting for yourself."

Leonard was quiet. He couldn't bring his eyes to meet Jack's; they flitted over his food, the airline catalog, his hands.

Jack returned to his dinner, but the food had lost its warmth and felt dry in his mouth. He set down his fork and chewed unenthusiastically.

WALK LONDON

Museums
Parks
Theatres
Restaurants
Shopping
Events

**Includes Tube Map
& Bus Routes**

COMPLIMENTS OF THE
BOND STREET
HOTEL

3

A CHANGE IN THE AIR

JACK'S ALARM SCREAMED IN HIS EAR LIKE A SIREN. HE batted at the snooze button to quiet it, then tried to focus his bleary eyes on the time. Two in the afternoon. His limbs felt like bricks, and he had no desire to get out of bed. But he knew he should if he wanted to beat the jet-lag effect of the eight-hour flight to Europe. Over the years he'd found that a four-hour nap, followed by an afternoon and evening of walking, was the best way to adjust to a new time zone.

He threw water on his face and looked in the mirror. He had a fair amount of stubble, but he decided to let it be. Today wasn't a workday, after all; it was a day for reacclimating himself to the city. It had been more than a decade since he had been in London.

The streets were busy with people, on their own particular missions. Jack was, too. He remembered a little café that served a delicious carrot-coriander soup. He couldn't remember the name of the café, or even the street it was on, so he navigated by instinct, pushing himself into his memories of his younger days.

Rounding the next corner, he saw a green canopy stretched out over a few white tables. This was it. The smell of buttery pastries drifted through the air. He couldn't help but feel a touch of emotion, a sense of connection to this place. It was exactly as he remembered it. But wasn't that the way of things in England? The country held fast to its history, even the little piece of his history.

There was quite a line at the counter, but he didn't mind. He was here as much for the atmosphere as for the food. It was small, but, as with so much of England, cluttered with many things. It gave the place a cozy feel. Jack looked around at the other patrons, people from all walks of life enjoying scones and cake. One couple in particular caught his eye; they were talking, laughing. The energy of young love shone on their faces, and they were oblivious to everyone but each other. His analytical reporter's eye could tell they were traveling on a tight budget: one cup of coffee between them. But he envied them.

He and Veronica had been this young couple once. Perhaps they had even sat where this couple were now sitting. Jack couldn't help but remember the excitement of traveling and exploring together. They were in their own little universe, just two people against the whole world. All of life was ahead of them. Their mission and purpose together were still unknown, but they were eager to discover it — together.

Jack shook the memories from his head. Young love, he reminded himself, is just the result of young chemicals coursing through young bodies. Nothing more, nothing less. And those feelings die with age.

But the nostalgia he was feeling, this sense of time standing still, made him wish for more. Was there something more? Was there a purpose beyond biology? Maybe it was their children. Were they the purpose? But they, too, would just grow up and be biologically attracted to some other young person. Was life just some meaningless cycle? If he was honest, that was exactly what he thought. But his heart wanted something else.

"Can I help you?" The elderly woman on the other side of the counter interrupted his train of thought.

"A bowl of carrot-coriander soup, to take away," Jack said. "And can you send a plate of scones and jam to the couple by the window?" he added on impulse. The woman looked at him a little strangely, but Jack was feeling better about himself already. Maybe being nice to people was what made the world go 'round.

Jack brought his soup to St. James Park. Spring was in the air. People were tossing around a Frisbee, others jogging. He made his way to the lake where kids were feeding the ducks. He saw families enjoying themselves, and older people holding hands. Maybe he should have moved with his family to England. There was a peace here that he had never seen anywhere else.

As he ate, Jack felt his discontent creep back into him. Maybe it was the jet lag — he was just out of his routine. On the other hand, maybe breaking routine had given him his first chance in a while to look around at the world. He was usually immersed in one story or another, questing after the truth as he saw it. He realized it didn't matter all that much; it wasn't much more than an elaborate game.

But at least it was an exciting game. And playing it, keeping at it, gave him a sense of purpose. Only — what if there was a purpose beyond just the sense of purpose?

Music began playing from behind Jack. He turned around to see a dozen people sitting on the grass with guitars, flutes, and other instruments. Those without woodwinds were singing along. He didn't recognize the song, but the scene reminded him of his college campus, where people would strum their guitars on the quad. He'd toyed with his roommate's guitar from time to time but never felt confident enough to play it in front of anyone.

Jack went back to his soup and listened to the music. It wasn't long before he realized that the group was made of Christians; he kept hearing words like God and glory float his way. Obviously they were out to evangelize the park. Jack smiled as he felt his journalistic impulses kick in; jet lag or not, he was ready to begin work.

He wandered closer to the group and listened as he finished his meal. He was surprised to find that older people seemed to be involved, and families. He was also surprised to hear them sing an old Beatles favorite of his.

"So is this some kind of band you have here?" he asked a few of them as the gathering began to break up.

"Oh, we wish," answered a forty-something woman holding a guitar. She laughed. "These are just music lessons."

"Your church has music lessons?"

"Our church?" she asked.

"I'm sorry," Jack stammered. "You were singing about glory and Jesus, so I assumed ..."

"No, this is just something our neighborhood decided to do. Some of the people here are Christians, but I'm not."

Jack frowned. "But you were singing about Jesus anyway?"

The woman smiled. "I want to learn how to play music. I want to spend time with my neighbors. What am I going to do, make people sign a 'no Jesus' contract?"

Jack laughed. "No, I suppose not." He stuck out his hand. "I'm Jack, by the way."

"Ingrid," she said, shaking his hand. "You know, three years ago I spent most of my free time driving to towns twenty miles away to find people I had things in common with. You know what that's like?"

"I do," he confessed.

"Then someone came along and pulled us together as a neighborhood," Ingrid said, "and I found out I have connections with people right around me. We have a lot of the same interests, and we learn from each other. I'm sure the Christians could have formed their own little group of musicians or organized their own barbecues, but I'm kind of glad to be a part of it all."

Jack left the conversation intrigued. He had expected to find that this Christian movement was the result of some church program that was growing larger and larger. But it seemed to have spilled over into the neighborhoods. Or maybe it had started in the neighborhoods. The puzzle was starting to intrigue him.

He remembered Westminster Abbey was nearby; it

had been a favorite sight of his when he was here last. It was a gateway to history. He could walk where famous kings once walked and where they now lay buried. He loved the symbolism of the two queens who hated each other in life now contained in the same small room. Shakespeare's statue honored the beauty of poetry and the endurance of art. There was this tangible connection to people whose legacies had shaped today's world. He could almost believe that the meaningless cycle of biology added up to something, some purpose beyond each individual's time on earth.

Jack neared the building, the sight of which still took his breath away. Stone block rose from the grass. Thick, massive walls held up heavy spires that stretched into the sky. This structure took some brute strength to raise up so many centuries ago. And although it seemed to Jack more a museum than a church, he couldn't help but admire the ancient faith of the ancient people who had built it.

However, he was here to investigate something new, something that was perhaps the next chapter in the story of this monument. Walking in, he resisted the temptation just to explore. He moved past a family kneeling and praying together, past a group of young people in their twenties singing together. They sounded pretty good in the old cathedral. Jack spied a man wearing an official-looking robe and angled his way toward him.

"Excuse me," he said, careful to keep his voice soft. "Are you a priest here?"

The man smiled politely. "A vicar, yes."

"I have some questions that I'd like to ask about, well,

recent developments in the church." Jack wasn't sure why he hadn't mentioned he was a reporter. Maybe he thought the vicar would be more candid talking to someone who appeared genuinely interested.

The vicar gestured for Jack to sit on a pew. "No problem. What would you like to know?"

"I hope this doesn't sound strange, but is there something new going on in the church? I don't just mean Westminster Abbey, but in London in general."

"I believe there is," the vicar said, smiling, "because people ask me this question every day. I've worked here at the cathedral for twenty-five years and have never seen anything like it. People ask me, 'Is it a fad of some sort? Is it of God?' and the truth is I just don't know. All I know is that I used to feel like a curator at a museum and now I feel like" — he laughed — "well, like a vicar at a church."

"So what is it?" Jack asked eagerly. "What's changed?"

"I wish I knew," the vicar said, deflating Jack's hopes of easy research. "But let me illustrate: Before this past year, do you know what the number-one question was from those visiting the cathedral? It was: 'Where did Elton John sing at the funeral of Princess Diana?'"

"Really! And now there's a new question?"

"Well, the American tourists still ask about the piano," the vicar said, smiling, "but people from England and some from the continent are starting to ask different questions."

"About God and the Bible?" Jack guessed.

"Well, I'd like to say that," the vicar said, "but they are asking more practical, logistical questions. Like, 'Where would be a quiet place for our family to pray?' Or — and this is really growing — people want to know when they can bring in a group from as small as two people to more than a hundred to sing." He gestured toward the entrance. "That group over there, for example."

"Yes, I noticed them," Jack said. "Is that some school choir or something?"

"No, it is just a neighborhood group that wanted to sing in a cathedral."

"But they sound so good," Jack said. "They know harmony and —"

"I was as surprised as you, at least at first. Now it's a regular occurrence. People are practicing in their homes and with their families. Friends come over, and they sing. It reminds me of the '60s and the music movement, except it's not just young people. Old and young, rich and poor — everyone seems to be singing and learning instruments."

"So it's a music thing," Jack said, almost to himself. "It's like karaoke, but carried to the next level."

"But it's not just music," the vicar said. "That's just the tip of the iceberg. People are hanging around, praying, getting in small groups and just talking. We have hundreds every day that just come in and read the Bible. Our few services at the cathedral, which had been mainly for show, are now attended by thousands every week. We don't have the staff to handle it."

"So where is all this interest coming from?" Jack asked. "Did the Church of England spearhead some new program?"

The vicar looked amused. "The Church of England has been built upon centuries of tradition, not on trying out new fads every ten years like the American churches. No, we have no idea where all this is coming from — and frankly, we are not sure what to think or do."

He leaned toward Jack and lowered his voice further. "There's a lot of chaos around here right now. To some degree, this trend is beyond our control. It's a little disconcerting to be wondering: What's next?"

Jack left the cathedral feeling a chill of excitement. He had expected to find behind this movement a tidy organization of evangelists armed with a new, methodical approach. Upon first encounter, though, he found it big, sprawling, and messy. As if infectious, it traveled the unpredictable web of human relationships — and left church leaders nervous over its next permutation.

With the sun beginning to set, Jack was eager to head back to his hotel and write up a few notes on his discoveries. He made his way to the Westminster tube station and snaked his way through hallways decorated with posters for West End plays. He followed signs toward the Jubilee Line and was waiting at the northbound platform when he noticed two familiar faces. The beautiful young couple from the café were standing nearby, arms around each other.

He smiled to himself and wondered if he should tell them he had been their mysterious benefactor this afternoon. He'd just decided against it when the woman looked over and caught him staring at them. He glanced away, embarrassed, but then decided to make the best of it.

"I'm sorry — I didn't mean to stare," Jack apologized.

"It's just that I don't see many couples as noticeably happy as you two."

"Thank you," the woman said, with a trace of a Dutch accent.

"Are you newlyweds?"

The husband shook his head. "We are married since four years ago."

"Really? That's inspiring," Jack said. He smiled at them and they smiled back. "I'm sorry, I haven't even introduced myself. I'm Jack, from New York."

"Gerrit," the husband said.

"And I'm Sofie. We're from Holland."

Jack looked at his watch, but the train was still a couple minutes away. "So, four years of wedded bliss, huh?"

Sofie and Gerrit looked at each other for a moment. Then Sofie looked up at Jack. "Actually, we are just now getting our marriage on track."

"Really?" Jack said, moving closer. "You seem so ..." He searched for the right words.

"Yes, I know. But a year ago at this time we called it quits." Sofie drew herself up. "Looking back, we were both in the marriage for ourselves."

Gerrit looked at his wife and nodded. "Each of us was wanting our own needs satisfied. Just take what we could get and never put anything in. We each knew something is wrong, but did not want to work on improvements."

Jack was increasingly intrigued. Maybe there was something more here than just hormones and biology.

"So what put you on track?" he asked.

Sofie smiled. "I was doing laundry in our flat, and I

started chatting with this older woman — well, in her thirties. I was complaining that Gerrit never helped with the laundry; in fact, I was nearly crying. So she asked me if I would be truly happy if Gerrit helped out with the clothes. In the end, I had to admit I wouldn't. I told her the real problem is that he's just so lazy about *everything*. She nodded and asked if I would be truly happy if Gerrit was just more responsible. I had to admit that wouldn't be enough. The fact was, I didn't know what I wanted out of marriage.

"But she seemed to know, and that made her intriguing. We talked all afternoon. She shared the story of her marriage; parts of it were just like ours. She invited us over to dinner, and we got to see what she and her husband were like together. We began to see in them what you see in us: life, love, purpose, God."

"God?" Jack said, drawing back a little.

"I know it sounds a bit weird," Sofie said, "but this couple had a strong relationship because they both had a strong relationship with God. Gerrit and I were not interested in God, church, and all that. Gerrit was raised with some religion but only casually. My family didn't bother. But we wanted what this couple had so much that we figured it couldn't do us any harm."

Jack didn't know about that. The last thing that would have helped him and Veronica was to paste on plastic smiles and sit in a pew on Sundays. Yet ... somehow, this God thing seemed to have worked for these people.

A metallic whine interrupted their conversation as the train entered the station, and the doors slid back for boarding. Jack followed Gerrit and Sofie onto the train. He was curious to know where their story would lead; it might even be relevant to his article.

"So this couple got you into religion?" Jack asked as they found adjacent seats.

"I would not say so," Gerrit answered. "It was more the little things at first: They show us how to read a Bible with each other. They show us praying. They let us try out that and then see for ourselves."

"We weren't sure exactly how it was supposed to work," Sofie said. "We felt a little silly. But in a few weeks we were talking like we never had before — talking about life, what we believed, what we feared. Our hopes, our expectations. It wasn't always pleasant. We fought about things we had never fought about before. I was scared. But our marriage became something we were both focused on again. We were thinking about an 'us' again, and wondering what our purpose was together." Sofie grasped her husband's hand and squeezed it. He smiled at her, then at Jack.

"Of course we could not have done it alone," Sofie continued. "Our sponsor couple invited us to meet other couples that were trying to do the same as us. We spent time together. We made meals and went places together. We helped each other. Soon our friends noticed that something had changed and began to ask questions. We just shared the truth. They were as skeptical as we had been — especially about the Bible stuff. We told them it was kind of like our international-cuisine nights: No one would force you to eat anything you don't like, but at the very least you have to taste and see."

Jack's mind flashed upon his conversation on the

plane. He'd told Leonard that you had to keep advertising hamburgers because they'd never changed anyone's life. But a changed life, on the other hand — maybe you could get away with 'Taste and see.'

"So did they take you up on the offer?" he asked.

"Actually, that's the reason we're in London," Sofie said. "We attended a big marriage-celebrating weekend."

"Twenty couples and we came over together who were each helped by our sponsor couple," Gerrit said. "I am quite surprised by the many people. Something to see."

A voice announced the next stop at Bond Street, and Jack stood up. "Well, it was very nice to meet both of you. I found your story quite interesting."

Sofie opened her purse and scribbled a name and phone number on a piece of paper. "Look, I know we just met, but you can call us anytime you need to talk about your marriage. We'll be home next week."

"Thanks, but I'm not married," Jack said, and smiled a false grin. Technically it wasn't a lie, but he felt extremely deceptive to have said it after how honest she had been with him.

He exited the train awkwardly and tried to push thoughts of Veronica out of his head. It was far too late for them to start over. Besides, he was here on business. He was doing research. He had a complicated story to unravel.

The *Global* J

100 W 41st St, Suite 3023, New York, NY 10

Jack,

Give me a call when you get a chance. I'd like t(
of how things are going.

[signature]

4

WHAT IS EVANGELISM?

JACK BLEW HIS NOSE LOUDLY INTO YET ANOTHER TISsue. He wasn't sure which he minded more: the stuffy pressure inside his head, or the rough tissues against his nose.

Hudson's voice boomed in his ear from 3,000 miles away. "So what kind of evangelism do they use?" he asked.

"Evangelism?" Jack spoke feebly.

"If the movement has grown as large and as quickly as you say, then they must have discovered some effective form of evangelism."

Jack sneezed again. "I don't think I've seen any," he said. "No one's accosted me with so much as a pamphlet."

Hudson chuckled. "Well, evangelism isn't always as brazen as that."

"Really?" Jack asked, intrigued. "I always thought the word implied a certain aggressiveness. At my old job there was this lady who was always pushing vitamins on everybody — we would call her the vitamin evangelist."

Hudson was no longer laughing. "I know what you mean. The sad truth is that even within the church, where we should know better, evangelism has this negative connotation of being a sales pitch. That's probably why so few people are interested in it, and even fewer follow through."

"So it isn't about twisting somebody's arm?"

"Of course not," Hudson said. "The word evangelism comes from a Greek word that means 'telling the good news.' It may take many forms, but evangelism is simply letting others know the good news of God's forgiveness. It's helping people take their first step toward God."

"Interesting," Jack said, considering the idea. "Then I suppose I have seen a form of evangelism."

"Great," Hudson said, his mood brightening. "Describe it to me."

Jack took a moment to find the words. "It seems that new people get interested because members of the movement are getting involved in their lives. These people have a big emphasis on getting together — to pray, to sing, to read the Bible, to learn, to eat together, to talk about their lives. The best I can figure it, the new people learn, by watching the old people, how to get close to God."

"Hmm — sounds like you're describing discipleship," Hudson said. "That's a whole different ball game."

"Discipleship?" Jack asked hesitantly.

Hudson chuckled again. "Sorry to keep dumping my Christian jargon on you," he said. "Discipleship is the next step after evangelism. First a person needs to come to Christ: We give a presentation or show a film, and we ask people to commit their lives to God. If they accept, then we begin discipleship — we show them what it means to live as a Christian. We teach them to read the Bible, get them into groups, get them involved in church, get them into classes."

Jack struggled to make sense of this. "I don't know,

Mr. Hudson. I've noticed a lot of the second part happening, but none of the first."

"What are you saying? That ... they're skipping evangelism? They're just discipling non-believers?"

Jack shrugged. "I can't really say. I'm not sure I understand the distinction between the two stages."

He heard Hudson open a drawer in his desk. "Well, the Bible is quite clear about the importance of evangelism — it's the very last thing Jesus said to his followers," Hudson said. Jack could hear pages of a book turning. "We call it 'The Great Commission' — here it is: 'Therefore go and make disciples of all nations, baptizing them in the name of the Father and of the Son and of the Holy Spirit, and teaching them to obey everything I have commanded you.'"

"I'm not an expert on this," Jack said slowly, not wanting to offend, "but Jesus didn't say 'go and evangelize.' He said 'go and make disciples.'" He felt a slight rush of warmth as he found himself engaged with this puzzle.

Hudson remained silent for several seconds. "I never noticed that," he said at last. "Of course, evangelism is implied. You can't very well disciple someone before you've won them over."

"You can't?" Jack said. "But that's exactly what I'm seeing here."

Hudson seemed to mull this over. "I've been getting ahead of myself," he said amiably. "Why don't you finish telling me what you've seen, and then maybe I'll have a better idea of their evangelism style."

Jack tried to think of a way to put his observations into words. His mind grabbed at a conversation he'd had yesterday with a young woman. She'd used a metaphor he hadn't understood at the time — but now it seemed quite relevant. "Is it common Christian jargon to refer to yourself as 'dating God'?" he asked.

"Not really," Hudson said. "The church is referred to as the bride of Christ, but that's as close as I've heard."

"The other day I met this woman who said she was not a Christian but she still attended the gatherings of the movement in her neighborhood. When I asked her why she bothered, she said she and God were still in the dating stage." Jack laughed. "It sounded a little weird to me; maybe because I'm a guy. But she went on to explain that she's still in the process of getting to know God. They've been introduced, she's spent a little time with Him, but she wants to know that she loves Him before she makes a commitment."

"Interesting."

"To be honest, I hadn't understood her metaphor until you mentioned 'winning people over.' That's the kind of evangelism I've experienced most of my life: People want to sign me up within the first few minutes that we meet." Jack hoped that hadn't sounded too insulting. "But here in England, it's more like — they just want to start me out on a blind date with God. They invite me to hang out with other people who are dating God or have gone on to marry Him. They talk about the ups and downs and the joys and frustrations of being with Him. But in the end, they seem to trust God to win me over in His own time."

"And this works?" Hudson said, sounding both skeptical and impressed. "But — without a commitment up front, how do they keep people coming back week after week?"

"I don't know — why to do two people decide to keep dating?" Jack asked. "I suppose it's because they're on a journey together. They're enjoying the process."

"Still ... it just seems like it would take forever to move a new person through that process. It's natural for discipleship to take a while, but evangelism has to be more direct."

Jack felt his spirits dampen. He was a writer, after all, but he couldn't seem to find the words to make clear what he had seen here. "Look, maybe you Christians get lost in your jargon sometimes," he said bluntly. "You try to draw a line between evangelism and discipleship, but they're not that different. They're both about helping another person get close to God."

Hudson cleared his throat, interrupting. "There is a line, though. One is for people who haven't committed to God, and the other for those who have."

"There you go, then — the main difference isn't what you do, only what person you do it to," Jack offered. "If the best way to grow close to God is by classes, groups, and prayer, shouldn't *everyone* use those techniques? Evangelism shouldn't look all that different from discipleship."

Hudson took a minute to continue the conversation. "I admit I don't understand this form of evangelism you're seeing," he said at last, "but I'm quite interested. Why don't you keep digging, tell me what you turn up, and maybe we'll discover a key to explaining it more fully."

Jack let out a raspy cough. As soon as he was back on his feet, it was time to step up his investigation a notch. It was time to find out what made these people tick.

THE FAMILY MEETING

1 Sing the song of the month!
Rate yourselves on a scale of 1 (needs work) to 5 (great): ____

2 Dig into the Word:
OPTION 1 — Read John 3 and answer the following questions as a family:

A) What does it mean to be born a second time?

B) Why did God send His Son into the world?

C) Why was John put in prison?

OPTION 2 — If you are each reading the Bible daily, discuss these questions:

A) What part of the reading was your favorite?

B) How did any of what you read influence how things went this week?

C) How did that impact your relationship with God?

3 Hospitality focus:
Decide as a family what can you do this week for your person/family of the month (see worksheet for ideas):

4 Review how well each person is doing at weekly goals.

5 Mission focus:
Help support your national church planter or missionary by choosing one activity from your mission worksheet.

6 As a family, plan the week's activities on the calendar.
Then, write down one special memory from last week that you want to remember:

7 Family offering:
Write down how much money you collected this week: ____
Decide as a family to whom you are giving it (see worksheet for ideas):

8 Recite the Bible verse for the month!
Rate yourselves on a scale of 1 (needs work) to 5 (great): ____

9 Answered prayer:
Look at prayer requests from previous weeks and write down any answers from God:

10 Family prayer:
This week, you are going to use the ACTS guide to prayer. Think of an item in each category and take turns praying out loud.

Adoration/praise:

Thanksgiving:

Confession:

Supplication/requests:

©2003 Bible League USA - www.bibleleagueusa.com

(29)

(To print out a sample of the Family Connection Planner, scroll to the bottom of the page)

HOW IT WORKS:

1. Sing the SONG OF THE MONTH!

2. DIG INTO THE WORD: Options are available for those who read the Bible daily, and for those who read one passage a week. Both options include a set of three questions for family discussion.

3. HOSPITALITY FOCUS: Decide as a family what you can do this week for your person/family of the month.

4. Review how well each person is doing at WEEKLY GOALS.

5. MISSION FOCUS: Help support your national church planter or missionary.

6. As a family, PLAN THE WEEK'S ACTIVITIES on the calendar.

7. FAMILY OFFERING: Write down how much money you collected this week, and decide as a family to whom you are giving it.

8. Recite the BIBLE VERSE OF THE MONTH!

9. ANSWERED PRAYER: Look at prayer requests from previous weeks and write down any answers from God.

10. FAMILY PRAYER: Rotating through prayer guides such as A.C.T.S., the Lord's prayer, and the Seven Connections allows you to think of an item in each category and take turns praying out loud.

5

CREATING A CULTURE OF EVANGELISM

THE STORY WAS NOT COMING TOGETHER. DESPITE HIS help from Hudson, Jack feared his lack of a Christian background put blinders on him. Every answer seemed to lead to three new questions.

He sighed heavily. If there was a common thread running through his research — a thin one, admittedly — it was the couple he was about to meet. More of his leads pointed to these people's door than any other — although, if he were honest, there were many leads that went elsewhere.

It was funny; for the fastest-growing church in England, it managed to stay fairly inconspicuous. The mainline churches were only vaguely aware of it. It wasn't home to a flurry of civic activities and meetings. Its handouts didn't even feature a slick logo. It was the people on the street who talked about it, who passed on stories of what happened there, who spoke of the leadership of Rev. Edwards and his family.

"Come by for supper," Edwards had said. He hadn't

wanted to meet at the church building — "Not much to see there, anyway."

So here Jack was, standing on the porch of a little townhouse just outside London, holding a bottle of sparkling juice. He was smart enough to know some Christian groups drank wine and some did not — why not play it safe?

The door opened and a young woman, balancing a child on her hip, greeted him. Behind her, a dog yipped a greeting as well.

"You must be Jack," she said. "Come on in. Don't mind the dog. Or the boy — neither one bites."

Jack smiled and followed her into the house. As he walked, he instinctively took in his surroundings. In the hallway he saw the usual collection of photos of grandparents, parents, and growing children — but they were arranged along the branches of a brown tree trunk painted on the wall. The frames and mats, he noted, were all green. In the main room he saw a well-worn drum in one corner, and in the other corner a miniature building project — an ancient temple or something. A set of crayon drawings hung around the room depicted bearded men in bathrobes. Scenes from Bible stories, he deduced. These people had things going on in their family.

"I'm Sue, by the way, and this young one is Kenneth," the woman said. The boy, who looked about three years old, buried his face in his mother's side at being introduced.

"Byron's going to be a few minutes late," she told him. "Understand that he doesn't normally do this — we like to be here for our guests. Hospitality is one of our themes around here." She pointed to a plaque that read: *Our family mission is to walk with God and share that walk with others through words, actions, and hospitality.*

"That's a great idea," Jack said. "It would give you something to strive for, I imagine. In my family, our only mission was to survive each other." He grinned.

Behind him, a girl's voice asked if he wanted any water or juice. Jack turned to answer, and saw that she was nearly the same age as his own daughter, nine or so. He was reminded of the prospect of missing spring break with Bethy, and his heart sank.

"Tell you what," he said warmly, recovering his smile. "I'll trade you this juice for some water." He held the bottle out to her.

"That's Charlotte," Sue said as her daughter took the juice to the kitchen. "Quite the little helper."

The two adults sat down and began talking about raising children, and Charlotte brought back two glasses of water for them. Kenneth began racing in circles to make himself dizzy.

"So ... you're a reporter, right?" she asked abruptly, her eyes betraying a sense of worry.

"That's right."

"Well, maybe I shouldn't say this," Sue said, "but we're a little nervous about your being here — about the publicity."

Jack frowned. "Why? Are you afraid I'll make you look bad?"

"No, we're afraid you'll make us look good."

"And why would you be against that?" Jack asked.

Sue concentrated on her drink, wiping condensation from the glass. Then she met Jack's eyes. "Because everything that has happened, all the good things, the thousands of lives that have been changed for the good — it has all happened without it."

Jack nodded slowly. "So why change the game plan now, right?"

"Yes, but it's more than that," Sue said. "I guess I, personally, would fear that if you write some favorable article, church leaders and pastors would start coming by to find our secret. They'd invite us to speak at their next conference on church growth. They'd reduce what is happening to some marketable format or formula."

Jack understood. "Like using the family mission, you mean."

"Exactly." Sue brightened. "It's not just one piece or another that makes a difference — it's a whole host of things that together make up our church culture."

"A culture?" Jack asked, but his question was drowned out by the dog starting to yip again. Jack and Sue turned to see Byron enter the room.

"Sorry I'm so late," Byron said. "We like to be here for our guests." He, too, pointed to the mission statement on the wall. Jack took note that he and his wife were consistent. "It's nice to meet you at last."

The two men shook hands, and Sue ushered the group into the dining room for dinner. Jack watched as Byron, Sue, and Charlotte brought out food from the kitchen and arranged it on the table.

"So tell me, Jack," Byron said, as he placed a salad on the table, "what do you do when you're not being a reporter?"

Jack had to think about that for a moment. "To be honest, I'm usually wrapped up with my job or taking the kids out somewhere. But I suppose you'd find me outdoors when I take time off. Fishing, maybe a bit of hiking. I like to take walks, get the blood pumping."

Byron sat down next to Jack. "Fishing, eh? I do a spot of fishing myself. Nothing like teaching your kids how to fish, is there?"

"Actually, I haven't taken them fishing yet," Jack said. "Bethy, that's my oldest, won't touch a worm, and Scott's still too young."

"No such thing as too young," Byron said insistently. "Kenneth here can't hold a rod or thread a hook, but he knows how much Daddy loves to fish. And when you get right down to it, that's the key to teaching someone how to fish. You share it with someone because you love it, and that's contagious."

Jack nodded, surprised at how much sense Byron made. He'd always thought he loved fishing just because he'd been doing it for so long, but it had been his grandfather who'd taught him. There'd been something so joyful about those summer weekends.

"Honey," Sue interrupted. "I think we're all set now."

"You know what that means, kids," Byron said. "Does everyone know the verse of the month?"

"Of course, Daddy," Charlotte answered, beaming.

Together, the four of them recited: "Mark 1:17 —

'Come, follow me,' Jesus said, 'and I will make you fishers of men.'"

Byron praised the kids for their efforts — Kenneth had remembered perhaps half the words — and then said grace for the meal.

Jack spent the prayer thinking about the Bible verse he'd heard. He could relate; he'd often felt like a fish that Christians were trying to hook. They'd dangle just about any kind of bait out there in order to stick him. Jack wondered what perspective Byron, as a fisherman, would have on it.

"Explain this idea of 'fishing for men' to me," Jack said casually, as he served himself a slice of beef Wellington. "Because a lot of times I feel like Christians are out to bait and hook me — it's like entrapment for sport."

Byron let Jack's question hang in the air momentarily. "It's a metaphor," he said at last, "and, like any metaphor, it can be stretched too far. The truth is, we've often treated non-Christians like fish, and we've used a verse like this to justify it.

"But let's place the statement in its original context. Fishing was not a sport 2,000 years ago; it was a trade. It was a livelihood. It was something that your father and grandfather had done before you, that you had been apprenticed in growing up. It was an identity. It was a passion. When Jesus comes along and says he wants to make Peter and Andrew into fishers of men, he was giving them a new identity, a new passion. He was giving them something new to pass down, to apprentice others in."

Jack passed the serving plate of roasted potatoes on to Sue. "So what's this new job look like?" he asked. "What does it mean to fish men?"

Byron took a sip of his sparkling juice. "The first three words of the verse tell us — Jesus says, 'Come, follow me.' He invites them to walk alongside Him, to be part of His life. He fishes them right out of their old life and into a new one. If there's any model for fishing men, it's right there: inviting others to walk alongside Jesus with you."

Jack chewed a bite of potatoes and tried to digest what Byron had said. He'd underestimated how interesting the Bible could be.

"So it's not about baiting anybody?" he said.

"Not at all," Byron answered. "A fisher of fish usually cares about catching something, but a fisher of men? He wants to pass something on."

Loud truck noises erupted from Kenneth's place at the table as he began driving a chicken strip around the edge of his plate. The conversation turned toward what was and was not appropriate for the dinner table, with Charlotte voicing the strictest position.

"So tell me, Jack, what would you like to know about our church?" Byron said. "What questions do you have for us?"

Jack brought his attention back to business. He put down his knife and fork and gathered his thoughts. "I know that you guys are reluctant to dissect this movement, and that no one part of it makes it work" — he nodded toward Sue — "so I'm not exactly sure where to begin my questions."

Byron smiled. "Personally, I'm curious to know what it looks like from your vantage point. What do you make of all this?"

"All right," Jack said. "It seems clear that wherever Christianity has been in the past, it is now struggling ... yet somehow your version of evangelism flourishes. I just can't put my finger on why. The most unusual thing I've noticed is that every single Christian I've talked to here — or at least 99 percent of them — has wanted to share something about their life with me. So is that the key: getting full participation from your church?"

"Interesting," Byron said, and paused to mull it over. "I can see how you would think that. Most churches have about five percent of people involved in evangelism, and we have nearly full participation, so it would follow that we would grow much faster. But no, I'm quite sure that full participation is a side effect of the movement, not its cause."

"How can you know?"

Byron talked as he cut his meat. "Think of it this way: If you lost a lot of weight eating a new miracle snack bar, you'd be pretty excited, right? You'd probably tell people about this snack whenever someone mentioned losing weight. You wouldn't be able to help yourself. But if someone came along and told you that you had to sell a case of snack bars to every person you met, you'd suddenly get really quiet about it. Almost all people are willing to talk about themselves — it's one of our most favorite subjects. But only about five percent of people are cut out to sell something."

"So you're saying the approach you use determines the participation you get," Jack said.

"Right — and I learned that the hard way," Byron said. "I have a seller personality, so for years I participated in all kinds of selling techniques: tracts, crusades, door-to-door evangelism, street ministries, dramas in the park, seeker-sensitive services, videos, literature, classes."

"I'm not exactly sure what all those are," Jack said tentatively.

"Well, don't worry about them," Byron said, waving the thought away with his hand. "The point is that I kept trying to get churchgoers to join me in these programs, and I found I could only attract certain personalities. The first kind were people like me, the born salesmen. We thrive on getting rejected over and over so that, when someone accepts, we experience a little high. Later on I realized that perhaps I was in evangelism for that little high I got.

"I could also attract the duty-bound personality. These types see the command in the Bible to go and share with others, and feel good about themselves only when they obey."

"That's my personality type," Sue offered. "I was doing evangelism because it relieved my guilt over a task undone."

"Right," Byron said, "most of us had some personal reason for selling Christianity. There were the social-butterfly people, who loved meeting new faces. Sharing Christ was a great excuse for them to engage with anyone, anywhere. Some people had a herd personality — they felt comfortable only in a like-minded crowd. They had to convince others to believe in order to feel secure about their own beliefs. Other people had a savior personality — they needed to rescue someone. These people did evangelism because of the great feeling of being needed. Last but not least, there were the enthusiastic people, who were often the newest people. They wanted to talk about the good news and good times to keep themselves upbeat and stoke the fire of their enthusiasm."

"May we be excused?" Charlotte said, spotting an opening in the conversation. Kenneth's chair was already empty, but Jack could hear faint truck noises coming from beneath it.

"Of course," Byron said. "Play in the lounge for a while until we're ready for the family meeting." Kenneth raced out of the room; Charlotte took her dishes into the kitchen.

Jack returned to his line of questioning. "So, if I understand correctly," he said, "selling is not the answer — it only works for the five percent who are wired to act that way. It doesn't work for the majority of Christians."

"Correct."

"So what's the alternative?" Jack asked. "In my interviews I get the feeling it has something to do with being open about your life, or with being friendly — but I can't seem to put my finger on it."

Byron thought about an answer. "It's not quite that simple. In recent years, something called friendship evangelism has become quite popular, and it utilizes friendliness and openness. But it the end, it is often a set-up for the sell. Instead of hitting up a stranger with a gospel presentation, you befriend the person — to soften up your potential buyer — before you unleash the sales pitch."

"OK, fine," Jack said wearily. "But that still doesn't tell me what the alternative is. If these other methods don't work, what's your method?"

"No method at all," Byron said. He smiled broadly. "I don't mean to be evasive with you, but this didn't start with me trying to figure out how to get evangelism going in our church. I never developed a curriculum or appointed a committee to discuss the matter. What happened is simply that my life was transformed by God."

He paused to finish the rest of his juice. "You see, my father and I fought constantly when I was growing up, and by the time I was eighteen I had moved out and barely looked back. Then my mother was diagnosed with cancer, and was given only a few weeks to live. I moved back into their house to help care for her, and a friend of mine — who became something of a mentor later on — suggested that this was my opportunity to heal my relationship with my father.

"I wasn't sure where to begin, or even if I wanted to begin at all, but this mentor suggested that my father and I take turns reading Psalms to my mum to comfort her. I didn't think he'd go for it, and I didn't think a few Bible verses were going to change anything between us. But he said yes. And before long it became impossible for me to hear those words of peace, and even the words of anger in some parts, coming from my father's lips and not begin to see that he was every bit as human as I was. And the wall between us just fell." Byron's lips trembled slightly. "I had thought the plan was to get him to change, but my mentor knew that we just needed God as a liaison between us."

Sue took over the story, having obviously heard it hundreds of times before. "You wouldn't believe the difference that made when he was talking to people. It was no longer 'you need this' or 'you should do that.' It was, 'God has made a difference in my life.' We were used to talking about the Bible as the source of all truth, but then it became 'The Bible helped heal me.'"

Byron had regained his composure. "The point is that sharing the good news has less to do with what I do to people — some presentation, some argument — and more to do with what I am doing in my own relationship with God, and whether that's worth copying. It has to do with the practices and habits in my marriage and my family that put God at the center of my relationships and bring us close together. Is my Christian life worth replicating?"

Jack wiped his mouth with a napkin. "I can see how that approach is different from selling," he acknowledged, "but it seems that you'd get maybe one percent of people following that course, not one hundred. You'd really have to have your act together before you could talk to anybody."

Byron shook his head. "You're still thinking of Christianity as a program to join, or as a system of thought to adopt," he said. "It's more like fishing for you and me — we might not be the best at it, we might not know all there is to know, but we love it. We'd love to teach others to love it, too. Christianity is just one of those things I love. I love God; I love how He's changed me; I love hearing how God interacts with other people. That's the atmosphere we have at our church. That's the kind of culture we cultivate. The evangelism is just a natural by-product of that."

Sue murmured her assent. "You see, if Christianity is something that is making a meaningful difference in your daily life, then average Christians will be able to get others excited about it. They won't be able to help it. But if Christianity is not making much of a difference in the lives of average people, then you have to constantly prop it up with marketing and selling."

Something clicked in Jack's head; he began to see a single thread linking all the stories that people had told him about their lives. They had all described an old life and then a new life. He smiled, glad to feel his intuition had not completely left him. "So your movement is driven by the engine of personal transformation."

Byron thought this over. "I suppose you could put it that way. It's the spark, at least, for getting the thing moving." He smiled. "Of course, without God at the steering wheel, it wouldn't move at all."

"Of course," Jack said, and returned the smile, although truthfully he was reluctant to assign God a role in any of this.

Charlotte came back into the dining room and asked if her parents were ready for the family meeting yet.

"Actually, we're running a little late," Byron said as he looked at his watch. He asked Sue to set up for the meeting while he and Jack cleared dishes.

Jack followed Byron into the kitchen with a stack of dirty plates. "I don't have to be here for this if you'd rather have family time alone," he offered.

"Nonsense," Byron said. "We invited you to our home not only to answer your questions about the movement, but to show you how it works. You did get the website address with the family-meeting pages, didn't you?"

"Yes," he said, "although I didn't really understand what they were for."

"Then let me show you," Byron said, and ushered him into the lounge.

Sue was on the couch, tuning a guitar, and the two children were sitting on the carpet. Byron joined his wife, and Jack remained standing in the doorway to watch the group.

Sue invited Jack to sing along with their song of the month, which was "Amazing Grace." He didn't know the words well enough to join in, but he enjoyed listening to the family's surprisingly melodic voices; it had been many years since he'd heard the familiar tune.

As the Edwards family moved on to reading a Bible passage and answering questions about it, Jack found himself tuning out the conversation and just taking in the happy interaction. He was homesick for his children already, but this made him wonder what kind of people he was raising his kids to become. He was always taking them to fun places on the weekends when he saw them

— probably to compensate for being away so much — but was he anything more to them than fun? What was he teaching them? Were they learning anything about life from him?

By the time Jack roused himself out of his thoughts, the group had moved on to discuss their mission focus for the week. Apparently they supported an African church planter, and the kids decided they wanted to make a card for him. As Byron brought out construction paper, crayons, and glitter, Jack decided he wanted to be part of this. He joined the kids on the ground and helped them with the glue stick.

An hour flew by as the family members gave out stickers for how well each person had done at chores, chose a person to be their hospitality focus next week, gathered coins and notes for a family offering, planned their activities for next week on the calendar, and made a list of the prayers God had answered for them.

Jack had felt comfortable throughout most of the meeting, but when they ended the evening by praying to God, he felt suddenly excluded again. God was OK as a topic of conversation, or even as a Higher Power that helped you out, but talking to this God person just seemed like hocus-pocus. If He was God of the Universe, He wouldn't be hanging on humans' every word, would He?

After the meeting, Sue took the kids upstairs to bed, and Byron led Jack into the kitchen for some tea and cake.

"So what did you think?" Byron asked.

"It was fun — a lot of good activities," Jack said. "But, to be honest ... I didn't see what it has to do with the movement."

"Well, it's simple, really. Our family meets like this every week. Our neighbors on either side meet, too. The staff at my church all meet with their families. In fact, the majority in my church have joined in — singles and couples make their own groups or join with nearby families and participate, too. We often gather as a large group to sing our songs or join together on a hospitality project. Our church gives special recognition to families that don't miss a meeting for a whole year. The family meetings are just part of our culture."

Jack stirred a little more sugar into his tea. "You've mentioned this culture thing a few times now, but I don't quite understand what you mean by it."

Byron nodded. "Take England, for instance," he said. "Our culture is very similar to yours in America, but you can definitely tell the difference when you're over here — the words we use, the way we drive, what we eat."

"Actually, I enjoy those little differences quite a lot," Jack said, smiling. "I feel like I'm fitting in a little when I say 'take away' in a restaurant instead of 'to go.' It's like a little game."

"Exactly. These minor differences are what give a culture its character, its personality. In my church's culture, we all have these family meetings. We have a culture of prayer. We have a culture of getting into the Bible — and, in turn, the Bible helps us further create culture. We have a culture of singing, of hospitality, of generosity. That's what it means to be part of our community."

"So you try to attract people with these little distinctions?" Jack asked.

"Well, I like to think that their primary purpose is to strengthen and enrich the lives of our members." Byron munched on a tea cake. "But, yes, we do want our culture to be attractive. We do make an effort to create an appealing community. Because in the end you can never accept *only* Christ — you have to accept Him and His family.

"A lot of evangelism is geared toward accepting a particular message or a particular belief, not a particular people. But you can't embrace God without embracing His people. It's like when my brother fell in love with an Indian woman in college. At first he was thinking just about her personality and her charm, but before long he realized he was getting himself involved with a whole new culture, a whole new set of rules and expectations, and a whole new set of people. Fortunately for him, he found this culture interesting, and now the woman is my sister-in-law. We hope to make our community interesting and attractive for the same reason — to draw others into it."

Byron sipped the last of his tea and continued. "The fact is, our church has no evangelism committee, no marketing department, no budget for tracts or literature. We do no real work on evangelism at all. We put all the real work into the culture, making it alive and powerful and binding. We make it into a breeding ground for changed lives. And we measure how well we're doing by how willing people are to share their walk with God. If our culture is really plugging people into a vibrant relationship with God, they'll talk about it. Word will spread. Evangelism will happen quite naturally."

Jack soaked in Byron's words. At last, it made sense why he'd scarcely heard the word "evangelism" since he arrived in England. No one here fretted about it; it was a natural by-product of vigilantly putting God at the center of everything in life.

Sue returned from upstairs and joined the men at the table. The children, apparently, had not wanted to go to sleep, and the conversation turned toward the frustrating yet adorable things that kids will do to evade responsibilities. Jack laughed as he shared some of his favorite stories about Scott and Bethy, although, in truth, his family arrangement made those moments bittersweet.

The evening grew late, and Jack decided to excuse himself. As Byron walked him to the door, Jack tossed out a last question. "By the way, when does your next church service take place? I'd like to take one in firsthand."

Byron just smiled. "I'm sure you've already been to one of our church gatherings."

"No," Jack corrected. "I've never even been to your building."

"That wouldn't be necessary," Byron said, shrugging. "We're not really a church that packs people into an arena. We have multiple, loosely connected things happening all over the city. You've probably wandered into one or two."

"Really?"

"Sure. There's actually a whole network of churches and gatherings that have spun from what we originally started. There are probably a hundred thousand people connected in some way to what we do."

"A hundred thousand?" Jack said, quite surprised.

Byron shrugged again. "Don't get the wrong idea — it's not like I'm actually in charge of that many people. I don't set the agenda for everyone, I just help coordinate everyone's efforts."

"Still — you said there were fifty or sixty people in your church ten years ago. That's incredible growth. Almost unbelievable, to tell you the truth."

"No, not really," Byron said, waving away the suggestion. "It may sound like a lot, but I don't think you understand how fast the good news can spread. Let's say it takes me an entire year to reach just one person. And the next year, each of us reaches just one more person apiece. At that pace, it takes only twenty years to reach a million people. In thirty years, the whole planet would be covered."

Jack shook his head in disbelief. "You make changing the world sound almost routine."

Byron laughed. "Pardon my nonchalance," he said. "I suppose if I felt I was responsible for the size of our church, I might be a little more impressed. But it's God's doing. And I know it's just the very start of what He has got in store."

Jack stared blankly. "Even considering that He's allowed Christianity to take 2,000 years to travel once around the globe?

"Ideas and beliefs always traveled slowly in the past," Byron said matter-of-factly. "There was little interaction between one nationality and another. Language barriers and prejudices kept people at arm's length.

Economic reality kept you in the same town you were raised in, and rigid social classes kept you from talking to half the people there. But in the last hundred years, barriers have fallen. We stay in touch with people all over the country and all over the world. Even though there are far more people these days, the planet is connected by just six degrees of separation."

"Doesn't that have something to do with Kevin Bacon?" Jack interrupted.

"Sorry?"

"Oh," Jack said lamely. "I heard about this game called 'Six Degrees of Kevin Bacon' — movie fans try to link the actor to any other actor through six films or less."

"Interesting," Byron said. "Well, what I'm talking about is similar in principle but of much more importance. It states that we're all just six relationships away from anyone else on earth. Free trade, air travel, media coverage, and computers have broken down boundaries between us. We've been linked together in a vast network."

Jack shifted his weight onto his other foot. "And this networked world is somehow better for spreading Christianity?" he asked.

"Not automatically," Byron said. He gestured back toward the lounge and invited Jack to sit down again. "In many ways, the networked world has created more hurdles for Christianity. Now that our circle of friends extends far beyond our neighborhoods, the church is no longer the default social and cultural center of town. New diversions and entertainments mean that it's harder to entice people under our roof. The typical church response has been to try to keep up with the competition. Especially in America, I've noticed, they've been building gymnasiums and softball fields, classrooms and auditoriums to keep the interest of those who like athletics, singing, intellectual study, and socializing. They're offering specialized programs for kids, families, men, women, couples, singles, teens, and the retired. But the fact is, no matter how hard Christians try, we can't compete with Hollywood for the best entertainment, with community centers for the best sports and crafts, or with vast libraries of books for the best spiritual insights.

"But in the movement, we make use of the networked world rather than fighting it. Instead of trying to bring the whole world under our roof to give them the good news, our church brings the good news wherever our people go — into neighborhoods, workplaces, sports programs, community activities, families — from one person, one couple, one family to another. The good news spreads across the network of humanity like a positive computer virus, infecting one person after another with the love of God."

Jack leaned back in his chair, absorbing Byron's words. This idea of a network gave a kind of structure to what he'd believed was a lot of random activity. It fit his research perfectly — people affecting people rather than disseminating some program.

"That's a great image," Jack said. "In a way, that's how I eventually discovered you — I followed the invisible threads of connection between people and found that a great number of them plugged in directly to you."

Byron waved the thought away. "I know this will sound like false modesty, but the network is much deeper than me. And I can trace my own spiritual influence back through a chain of at least eight people. Who knows if these threads of connection go back even further, or where they all converge?"

Jack was surprised by how deeply this thing went. It really seemed to be a grassroots kind of effort. "Do you think I can get in touch with that eighth person in your chain?" he asked, casting his hook for an interview.

Byron yawned. "I don't know — it was several years ago when I last saw him. I'm not sure I even have his number anymore."

Jack nodded, expecting as much. It was just as well; he had enough good information from this evening to begin putting together his article. If things went well this week, he might make it home for spring break after all.

last place on earth I'd expect to see this happening," says Pithers. "You have to understand: Our famous British reserve and polite formality should have nipped this thing in the bud. People here just don't go around talking about their marriage problems or their personal struggles. Or, at least, they didn't used to."

Dr. Bertenshaw also struggles to understand. "I would sooner have expected people to start weaving tapestries or donning suits of armor than for the Church of England to be showing so much life. Don't get me wrong — people here have always taken an interest in church, but mostly within the context of our heritage and identity as British citizens. I always expected it to stay there."

However, despite the obstacles of sedentary tradition and proper manners, the church movement is growing exponentially. London is perhaps the epicenter of this quake, but reverberations are felt as far away as Exeter, Shrewsbury, and Newcastle, not to mention continental cities like Brussels and Paris.

The key to success seems to lie in the power of a changed life. "Once your life has been transformed," says Rita Fairbanks, West Yorkshire resident, "you want to share it. Once your family has been transformed, you want to share it. Two years ago I used to fight with my daughter constantly; now I have a natural bridge to help other struggling parents. What am I supposed to do, just keep silent?"

With more than a million other enthusiasts thinking the same thing, England is poised to become a very loud place indeed. The only question is: Will their magic continue to change lives, or will the clock strike midnight on this Cinderella tale?

6

GETTING TO KNOW GOD

JACK RAN HIS FINGERS THROUGH HIS HAIR AND PRESSED his forehead into his palm. He stared gloomily at the screen of his laptop and read the ending of his story for what seemed like the thousandth time. There was something missing there, something elusive.

He heard a knock at the door to his hotel room. It was almost eight o'clock; it couldn't be the housekeeping. No one else knew he was here, so it had to be a misguided guest. He tried to settle back into his thoughts, but the knocking continued.

"Who is it?" he asked, grabbing his dress shirt off the bed and pulling it over his sleeveless undershirt.

"Mr. McClellan?"

"That's me," he answered cautiously. "Who are you?"

"Alec Davenport. You wanted to talk to me."

The name meant nothing to Jack. He went to the peephole and saw an older gentleman, nearly bald, who wore thick black glasses. He wore a charcoal suit and a lop-sided smile.

Jack unlocked the door and opened it partway. "Do I know you?" he said.

"Pastor Edwards told me to come see you," the stranger said. "He mentioned you were asking about me."

"Asking about you?" Jack said, confused.

"Yes, I'm Byron's ... well, I'm not sure what the word is. Perhaps his great-great-grand-mentor?" The corners of his eyes twinkled.

Jack laughed. "I remember. You're like the grandfather of the movement, right? Come on in, take a seat." He ushered his guest to the desk chair and took the edge of the bed for himself. "So you must have watched this movement from its beginning, haven't you?"

Davenport shook his head. "It didn't work that way. I didn't know what was going to happen. I was just helping some friends with broken marriages to listen to God. It wasn't until years later that I even found out I was connected to this whole phenomenon."

"Still, that had to feel pretty good when you did find out."

Davenport shrugged. "I suppose. But I can't really take credit for anything. Byron used to insist that I was the founder of the movement, but I don't think God works like that. God speaks to many people when He speaks."

"What do you mean by that?" Jack asked.

"If you or I could really see the whole picture, I think we'd find that God inspired many people with the same idea," Davenport said. "A little trickle starts in one place, another trickle starts somewhere else, and eventually all these trickles converge with each other. God does use leaders to pioneer new directions, but there is never one king-pin. There's never one founder." He shook his head gently. "We have such a desire to make gods out of men."

Jack nodded. "So what has your perspective been on this whole phenomenon? If not as a founder, then what?"

"I'm sure Byron gave you the leadership perspective already. I'm still down in the trenches. Ask me anything about the movement at the face-to-face level."

"Sure," Jack said vaguely. He'd conducted hundreds of such interviews, and had all the material he needed. Or maybe not — there was still the missing piece to this puzzle of a story. He was struck by how serendipitous it was that Davenport had shown up just now.

"Actually, I have just the question for you." Jack leaned forward and grabbed a pen and Steno pad from the desk. "OK — I understand that once your life has been transformed you want to share it. I understand that if your marriage or your family or your job is transformed that you want to share it. But what I don't understand is why anyone's life transforms. I mean — praying? singing? doing things with others? — I can see how they might make you feel better, but how does it change you? Is it all just psychology and therapy, or is there something of essence here?"

"It would be quite simple to tell you the answer." Davenport cleared his throat. "But it would be altogether more interesting to show you."

Jack felt a chill, which he ignored. "All right. I'm up for it."

"Then tell me," Davenport said. "What is your spiritual dream?"

"My spiritual dream?" Jack asked. "What does that mean?"

"Whatever you think it means," Davenport said calmly.

Jack did his best to keep from rolling his eyes. He searched his mind. He supposed his visitor was talking about whatever it was he wanted deep down. "To be closer to my two kids," he said at last. As he spoke, it occurred to him that he had promised to call them last night. Veronica was not going to let him forget that. "And a better relationship with their mother, I suppose."

"Good. What else?"

Jack closed his eyes and thought. He remembered his visit to the pastry shop his first day here, and how homesick he felt for that time in his life when he had something in life to look forward to. "I guess I want a sense of real purpose, as if life meant something."

Jack looked at Davenport, who continued to stare at him. Jack filled the silence. "I want to know what life is, what my part is."

"Yes, I would have guessed," Davenport said at last.

Jack felt toyed with. He hadn't even known himself what he was going to say until it popped out of his mouth. "God told you so, I suppose."

"No — though you would be surprised what God does tell you," Davenport said. "It's just that I've asked this question of so many people, and most tend to give the same two answers."

"Did I do that?"

Davenport smiled. "Well, you be the judge. Most people have what I call the God answer. They want to know the truth about life, and their place in it. They want to be connected to whatever universal power exists. One American I met told me he wanted to be one with the whales."

"One with the whales?" Jack said with a poker face.

"Indeed. Think about it: Some people believe that we are all a part of God — that nature is part of God. He was really saying he wanted to be one with God."

"All right. So what is the second answer?

Davenport adjusted his glasses. "Most people have a dream of making a difference in the life of family members or friends. It seems most of us want to have made a positive difference in the life of someone while we are on this planet."

Jack felt transparent, having given such obvious answers. On the other hand, he felt pleased to find out that most of the world was in the same boat with him. "Well, that's interesting," he said, "but why is it important?"

"The truth is," Davenport said, "these two things that most people want are exactly what God wants for us. In fact, he commands them. Do you know the Ten Commandments?"

"I haven't got them memorized if this is a test, but I've read them once or twice."

Davenport grinned. "No test. A review. If you were to read them again you would discover that the first four commandments deal with our relationship with God. The next six deal with our relationship with others. That is why Jesus could summarize the ten into two: 'Love the Lord your God with all your heart,' and 'Love your neighbor as yourself.' See, God wants for us what we already want. Our spiritual dream and His are the same. It is as if every human being is born with a hand reaching up to God — whoever or whatever God is — and a hand reaching out to others."

"OK, I get that, but then why don't all of us achieve our dreams?" Jack asked.

"Well, something gets in the way."

"Let me guess," Jack interrupted. "Is it sin?"

"Yes," Davenport said, surprised. "How did you know?"

"In my experience, Christians eventually like to talk about sin," Jack said.

Davenport stumbled over his words slightly. "Well, yes, indeed. Do you know the Christian view of where sin came from?"

"Adam and Eve. They ate the apple."

"The fruit tree, yes," Davenport said. "And do you know what two things they did after eating the apple?"

"Not really," Jack said. "It's been a while."

"First they hid from each other — the whole fig-leaf thing."

Jack nodded with a smile.

"Then, as Genesis 3 tells the story, when God came walking through the garden in the cool of the day, Adam and Eve hid in the bushes." Davenport leaned toward Jack. "You see what is going on here? Most people have a dream to connect with other people — a friend, a spouse, their family — but sin is the relationship killer that keeps us from getting what we want. Most people want a connection to

God, but when He comes around, sin keeps us hiding in the bushes.

"People don't like to talk about sin," Davenport said, "but sin is just the general term Christians use to refer to all the things we do that break, tear down, destroy our relationship with God and people. The lies, the betrayal, the jealousy, the gossip, the selfishness, the pride, the envy — most everyone would agree these are damaging acts."

Jack eagerly jumped in. "Actually, that's exactly what I believe. What you call sin I call selfishness, and what you call goodness I call selflessness. Life is just a matter of tipping society toward the selfless."

"Yes, but you're forgetting that sin leaves wounds," Davenport said. "If someone stabs you in the back on an assignment, yet acts selflessly toward his family, you still feel wronged. You still feel angry. One can't heal the other; they don't cancel each other out."

"So what can we do about it?" Jack asked.

"Nothing."

"You're joking, right?" Jack said. "Doesn't forgiveness fit in here somewhere?"

"Yes," Davenport said, "but a person can't just manufacture forgiveness. If you feel wounded and full of hate, you can't just flip the forgiveness switch, can you?"

"I suppose not."

"That's why we need grace," Davenport said. "Forgiveness doesn't work without grace. Relationships can't work without grace. We're helpless — or we were until Jesus came into the picture. He makes grace a possibility by taking our guilt. That is what the cross is all about.

He took on the guilt of our sin."

Jack's mind struggled to connect the dots. "So, essentially, God kicks off a chain reaction of forgiveness: Once my guilt is taken away, I have the goodwill to forgive those who have wronged me."

"Exactly," Davenport said. "But it's not just about evening up scores. The vast, selfless love of God will fill us up and give us reservoirs of love to extend to the people around us."

Jack understood guilt rather well, but love ... . "That sounds a bit like you've entered flower-child, hug-a-tree territory."

"Not at all. Have you ever been in love, Mr. McClellan?"

"Yes," Jack answered after a slight hesitation.

"And when you found out that someone loved you," Davenport said, "did you not begin to see yourself through those eyes? Did you not begin to see others with the same generosity of spirit?"

Jack tried to recollect what it had been like to be happy with Veronica, but a much more recent event jumped out in his mind: Only three weeks ago he'd bought lunch for a pair of strangers solely on the memory of having been loved.

"I suppose that's fair to say," Jack admitted. "But knowing that a person loves you and knowing that God loves you are two different things, aren't they? I mean, I can see and hear and feel a person, but with God — well, how do this grace and this love actually get to you? How is your heart supposed to change, exactly?"

"In a nutshell?" Davenport said. "The Holy Spirit."

Jack thought for a moment, then shrugged. "I'm afraid you're going to have to crack open that nutshell for me."

Davenport laughed. "All right. Have you ever heard of John 3:16? It's probably the best-known verse in the Bible."

"Sure," Jack said. "There's this crazed man in the U.S. who used to go to all the sporting events with a big sign: 3:16."

"'For God so loved the world that He gave His one and only Son, that whoever believes in Him shall not perish but have eternal life,'" Davenport quoted.

"Yes, that's it," Jack said. "I've heard it here and there."

Davenport nodded. "This is a favorite passage of many when trying to convert someone."

Jack stared skeptically at the old man. "So are you trying to convert me?"

"No, I cannot convert you," Davenport said. "No, I bring up John 3:16 because I want to share with you a lesser known verse just a bit ahead — John 3:8: 'The wind blows wherever it pleases. You hear its sound, but you cannot tell where it comes from or where it is going. So it is with everyone born of the Spirit.' I cannot convert you because neither you nor I can control the Spirit of God any more than we can control the wind."

Jack still felt defensive. "If that's true, then how come I got bushwhacked on my plane ride by some guy trying to evangelize me?"

Davenport sighed. "Let me see how I might explain it.

Though you and I do not control the wind, we usually know where we can find a windy place, right? In the States, for example, where would you take someone to experience some good old Yankee wind?"

"Chicago," Jack replied. "The windy city."

"Here in England I would take you to the straits of Dover," Davenport said. "The point is that we know the place to bring someone to have a good chance of experiencing the wind. So, too, with God's spirit. Though we do not control the Spirit, we can know where the wind of the Spirit often blows."

Jack thought for a moment. "So you're saying that I can hear and feel God, in a way, but first I need to know where to look."

"Indeed."

"So where is this place?" Jack asked.

"That is a good question," Davenport said, "one which different churches and brands of churches have differing opinions about. Some think the windy place is knowledge. You need to learn this and that about the Bible, God, doctrine, church history; the more you know, the better the chances the wind will blow. Others think the windy place is commitment. You need to make a verbal vow of belief, and if you do there is a good chance the wind will blow."

Jack folded his arms across his chest. "That's where I felt the guy on the plane was coming from. I guess that's what my stereotype of Christians is. They always want you to pray to receive Christ."

"Yes, well, this is a popular view of where the wind blows," Davenport said. "Other brands of the church believe more in experience. You need to experience dramatic things, and those interested in evangelizing you will try to get you to experience these things. And still others believe the windy place is found in ritual and tradition: Do these things. Involve yourself in these rituals. This was the church I was raised in."

"So, who is right?"

"Well, this is what different churches often disagree over," Davenport said.

Jack smiled at the evasive tactic. "Then who do you think is right?"

"All of them," Davenport said, and the twinkle returned to his eyes. "Tradition, ritual, commitment, experience — they are all right, because all are part of a bigger thing: a relationship."

"I'm not sure I follow."

"What God wants most is to have a relationship with you," Davenport said. "He wants that with every person. He is reaching out to us with love not because He wants us to feel better about ourselves — nor to hear us grovel about our unworthiness. He has extended this hand of grace toward us so that we can take it in our own and walk alongside him. He wants the back and forth, the give and take, the excitement and discovery inherent in any good relationship."

"Like dating," Jack said, remembering the metaphor he'd discussed with Hudson.

"Indeed," Davenport said, smiling. His eyes softened. "I can still remember the first time I saw Edie — of course, I had no relationship with her yet. But I knew I wanted one.

We talked and listened. Before long, we began the ritual of dating. I acquired some knowledge of her and a bit of experience of what she was like, so I continued the dating ritual for about a year. Finally, after plenty of ritual, I had enough knowledge and enough experience that I made a commitment to her."

Davenport's face darkened. "But, as I said, the tendency is for people to favor one emphasis over the others. I leaned toward ritual; as long as I bought Edie flowers once a week, I figured I was a pretty good husband. I forgot that ritual was just one aspect of a whole relationship."

"And you're saying people do that with God?" Jack asked.

"All the time," Davenport said. "That windy place I was talking about — the place where the Holy Spirit delivers the grace won on the cross of Christ — isn't in ritual, experience, commitment or knowledge. It's in relationship with God. And you have to understand that God can't be boxed into a corner. That relationship may grow and change over time and lead you in new directions, and you need to keep following the wind."

Jack shook his head. "You know, I still can't picture it. If God is all He says He is, how can a human being carry on a relationship with Him?"

"Same as any other relationship," Davenport said. "Talk and listen. Talk and listen."

"But that's too simple," Jack said flatly.

"Simple to begin, yes. You and I have started a relationship here tonight without much effort. But to keep up a relationship through life's ups and downs — that is more complicated. You will fail at times. However, the beauty of walking with God is that He will always take you back. A person might have to break a relationship with you, but God has limitless love for you."

Jack trembled slightly. His eyes darted around the largely empty room, and he realized how lonely and barren his life was. He had cultivated it, hadn't he? The life of the reporter, always on the go, always involved for the short term. After Veronica, he had made sure never to be put in the position of being rejected again. He hadn't even realized how much he'd missed the reciprocal feeling of being needed. He shook again.

"A little chilly in here, isn't it?" Jack said, smiling apologetically. "These old English hotels have no insulation." He took a sweater from the dresser and put it on. "So tell me more about starting this relationship with God: Talking and listening — how does it work?"

Davenport scratched at his chin. "Well, talking with God is fairly straightforward: Christians call it prayer, and what you usually do is just unburden your heart like you might to a best friend. Everything that's going on that's important to you is important to God. It can be difficult at first, so I often teach a person who is just starting to talk to God to use a prayer guide.

"As for listening," Davenport said, "it's a bit more complicated. It requires tuning one's ear to God's voice, because it's not the same as a human's. The most consistent, trustworthy way to listen to what God is saying is by reading the Bible. God can speak to us in many ways, but the Bible is the standard we measure all messages against."

"And this really works?"

Davenport shook his head. "It is not the Bible reading and prayer that work. These are just the means of starting a relationship with God. It is the growing relationship with God that works."

Jack smiled. "Right, but still — do people really stick with it long enough to develop a relationship? I mean, I've taken a shot at reading the Bible before — someone told me it was the basis of all Western history, language and art — but I found it dry as dust."

"I'll be the first to admit that — although the Bible has been the number-one bestseller every year since the invention of the printing press — it is not the best read," Davenport said. "You are not alone in struggling with it. However, the Bible was not written to be read alone. Christianity is a way of life, a culture, a community. The Bible was written to be read and studied and lived in community.

"That lesson, sadly, took me many years to learn. I did not understand the power of this book, these words of God. Sure, I could preach them from the street corner and debate them in the classroom, but I never really thought of Bible-reading and prayer like sitting down and talking with a friend. I never read the words wondering why God put those words in front of me today. It was a textbook from which to extract truth — not a relationship-builder."

Davenport looked down at the carpet. "So, to my great shame and loss, I rarely opened the Bible together with my wife. Here was my wife — the most important person to me in the world — and over here was God, the other end of my spiritual dream." He held his hands apart as far as they would reach.

"I never sat down with both her and God together to just talk and listen. You know, I almost lost her." His lip quivered. "Not only her, but my whole family. I was so busy with church, so busy trying to get people to believe — because that's what I thought John 3:16 was about. *You have to believe. Do you believe this truth or not?* But you know what? The word 'believe' could be translated 'trust.'

"In my loneliest hour, sleeping on a camp bed in my brother's garage, God revealed that to me. This Christianity is not so much believing in truth as trusting in God. Trust is about relationship. Belief is about truth. I was way into truth, but way out of it when it came to relationships."

"So what did you do?" Jack asked.

"I started reading the Bible with my wife," Davenport said. "Our life together became our focus. It wasn't easy to rebuild, but with God in our corner I felt we had a fighting chance. Then we started reading the Bible and praying with our children. Over time, with God in the middle of our family, a God who wants our best, things began to improve.

"We grew quite excited about the changes in our family. We started sharing our story. We started inviting others to support us in our new walk. As we all read the Bible and talked with God and each other, a new, exciting culture started to take root. It was a Christian culture — a community bound together with habits and customs and rituals that joined people to each other and to God. Christianity, I discovered, was not just a set of beliefs or some philosophy of life that one can either accept or reject. It is the way we do marriage, the way we do family, the way we do friend-ship, the way we do business, the way we do music and art, the way we do social work. It is all of this inspired by our relationship — the relationship we have together with God."

As Jack listened, he was connecting Davenport's descriptions to people he'd met over the last four weeks; he could attach names and faces to each category. It nearly escaped him that Davenport had at last answered his question.

Jack grabbed his discarded Steno pad and began scribbling notes on it. He could feel the end of his article rewriting itself. "So the thing that animates all your activi-ties and gatherings and singing is this relationship with God," he said excitedly. "That's the glue that keeps the whole thing together."

Davenport smiled. "Yes. This is the core message of the Bible: 'God wants a relationship with you.' The good news of Jesus is simply that: 'You belong. You belong to God; you belong to these people; you have a place at the table.'"

Jack jotted down a few more notes, then stopped. "So why can't Christians just say that? Why do they have to evangelize using all these pat-answer formulas?"

Davenport considered the question. "Years ago, when I was using a lot of these formulas, I would have told you it was of utmost importance that I make a clear presentation of the Gospel. It wouldn't do for me to just talk about my own relationship with God, because I might obscure my clear presentation: usually done in one sitting to make sure everything was explained as a whole.

"But these days I would say: When is my presentation clear — when it's clear to me or when it's clear to the person I'm talking to? Because few people really understand something clearly the first time they hear it. People have to bump up against a new concept for a while, absorbing a new piece of information here and there before it starts to become more comprehensible. The conversation we had tonight wouldn't have made any sense to you when you first arrived in England; it's only by having seen and experienced and explored over time that the movement finally makes sense to you."

The words had the ring of truth in Jack's ears, and yet he knew from making his living telling stories that you usually get only one chance to hook someone's interest. Something had to grab people's attention before they would make an effort to understand.

"So how do you go about evangelizing?" Jack asked. "Do you just hope that sooner or later a new person will catch on?"

Davenport shook his head. "People tend to think along the lines of polar opposites: 'I should either convert someone in one sitting, or just sit back and let my life do the talking for me.' The key word to remember is relationship: Treat the other person as a human being to walk alongside and make part of your life."

Jack wrote again in his notebook. "But won't that limit the number of people you can evangelize? I thought the idea was to reach the 'ends of the earth' or something."

"True, but again people tend to go to polar extremes,"

Davenport said. "The traditional idea of evangelism tells you to fly off to Africa for a missions trip or go serve at a soup kitchen. It makes you feel good because you spent a lot of time, money, and energy on something. But most times it's energy wasted because you didn't make a relationship with anyone, didn't show people that they had a place at the table. The counteracting form of evangelism defines our mission field as our own backyard. We pour time and money into church programs and special events to draw people into our backyard. But, again, it's a lot of energy wasted, because so few people are brought in through such a gigantic enterprise.

"I think it's helpful to stop thinking geographically and start thinking in terms of natural bridges you have to people. Maybe you need to go to the soup kitchen because you were once poor and destitute yourself. You have a heart for these people, and you have some credibility in their eyes. Or maybe you really like playing sports, and you get along with that crowd. Instead of joining the church softball team, join your town's team and make friends there. Everyone has life experience and interests that give them these natural bridges toward befriending others, and that's your real circle of influence. You can't put it on a map."

Jack stopped writing. "I'm not sure you've answered my question. You've told me which people you evangelize, but not necessarily how you go about it. Do you just start talking willy-nilly about windy places?"

Davenport smiled. "Actually, I hesitate to define it for you. If I analyze the process too much, it risks turning rigid and wooden. It should come naturally, easily, spontaneously. But I think it really comes down to sharing what you've been saved from."

"I thought Christians were supposed to be saved from sin," Jack said, slightly unsure of himself.

"Yes, but which sin?" Davenport said. "And what circumstances were changed because of it? As for me, I was saved from the sin of religious effort, the sin of pride. And being freed from that helped save me from a poor marriage and a poor family. These are things that many people struggle with; I am never at a loss to share the story about how accepting God's grace remade me. I think the key to evangelism is that it has to spring out of your own story."

Jack mulled this over. "But you happen to have a particularly amazing story. Not everyone can have that."

"I'm glad you brought that up," Davenport said. "For many years I had trouble talking about my faith because I thought that being saved had something to do with the week I spent at a Christian camp in my early teens, where I made a commitment to God. Most Christians think the only salvation story in their life is the very first one. But I always ask people: What has Jesus freed you from recently — grief, addiction, temper, pride, selfishness, lust, little white lies, spectator faith? If people can't come up with an answer, I suggest they go out and get saved from something! A Christian in an active relationship with God will continue, throughout life, to be freed from new sins and new pains. Any of these stories are a valid entry point to talking about how God has rescued you. But you have to take a good look at your life and figure out where those stories are.

"The other step you have to take is to determine how you got from point A to point B. Most people aren't really aware of the process; they just know that it happened. Or, if they do chart the course, they focus on the big miracles and unusual circumstances, which a new person cannot hope to duplicate. You have to look at the most basic elements of the process — elements not unique to your circumstances but universal to God's dealings with humans. And I've found that, in every case, spiritual transformation was the product of talking to God and listening to God repeatedly. It's that back and forth of relationship. So evangelism, while it springs from your story, isn't dependent on the strength of your story. It's dependent on showing someone the ropes of handling a relationship with God."

Jack continued to jot down notes on what Davenport was saying, filling his tenth page of scrawl. He would have to work very late tonight in order to finish his article before his flight home in the morning. An unsuppressed yawn overtook him at the thought.

"My goodness, it is late," Davenport said, looking at his watch. "I didn't mean to keep you this long." He stood up very slowly, and Jack realized how much he must have tired out the old man.

"It was well worth the time," Jack said. "I feel like I'm finally getting a handle on what this movement is all about."

"Perhaps." Davenport smiled wryly. "A philosophical understanding of things is nice, but from day one you've known what this movement is about: people reaching out to you, inviting you to spend time with God."

Jack smiled back. "Perhaps," he admitted.

Davenport leaned his hand on Jack's shoulder. "I've been where you are, Jack. I know what it's like to keep an arm's distance from people. You're afraid that maybe your wife is right, that deep down you're as bad as she thinks, and no one else is going to get the chance to find out."

Jack didn't say anything. He felt an impulse to protest, but something held him back.

"There are a lot of people who want to get to know you. They want you to get to know God, too. And the good news is, God already knows how bad you are and He forgives you anyway. There's no risk. Spend a little time with Him and find out."

Davenport smiled, and Jack felt a business card pressed into his palm. "There are people willing to show you the ropes."

THE SPORTS EMPORIUM
PICCADILLY, LONDON

---

1 DELUXE TACKLE BOX, GREEN £ 7.95
1 PACK 6 FLOATS, GREEN £ 2.95
1 TELESCOPING ROD, GREEN £ 17.95

TOTAL DUE £ 28.85

PAID CREDIT CARD ************9837
MCCLELLAN, J   10 APR   08:21

THANK YOU FOR YOUR PATRONAGE!

THE SPIRITUAL DREAM

SUNLIGHT STREAMED THROUGH THE TINY AIRPLANE window onto Jack's tray table. He fidgeted with Davenport's business card, flipping it over and over like a flash card, as if the next time he flipped it he'd find the answers to his life printed on the back.

Even before last night, Jack had decided his life needed changing. He was leaving New York. Spending a week with Scott and Bethy shouldn't be the rare event he'd made it. There was so little time left to pass something on to them — his love of writing, his passion for fishing. He wanted to be a bigger part of their lives, even if it meant getting along with Veronica somehow.

And yet, had Davenport been right in calling this a "spiritual dream"? Did it require something more than his good intentions and his best efforts? Were all those Christians right in saying that only God enabled them to change?

Jack couldn't believe he was entertaining the possibility. Why would the Creator of the universe, if that's what He was, care whether Jack McClellan had a direction in life? He looked at the empty seat next to him, almost hoping to find a Leonard there he could refute with logic and reason.

Instead he only heard Davenport's last words to him. "The onus is on you, Jack," the old man had said. "No one is pushing you, no one is holding your hand, or making you jump through hoops. The only one holding you back is yourself. You haven't yet answered the big question: Do you want a relationship with God?"

The truth was, he didn't know. He'd never thought of God as anything more real than Mother Earth or Father Time — just a convenient metaphor for cosmic forces. Did God really have thoughts, feelings, and interests? How fully could a person really understand this God? How fully could a person trust God?

He couldn't say. But — as he gazed out his window over the shimmering waters of the Atlantic — he decided it was a story worth investigating.

"And the Word was made flesh,
and dwelt among us ... ."

— John 1:14 (KJV)

POSTSCRIPT

THE BOOK YOU'VE JUST READ IS REALLY FOUR DIFFER-
ent books. Depending on who you are and why you read
it, you will have one of four different perspectives on the
story. I would like to conclude with a personal note to
each of you.

To those who felt evangelized:

Perhaps you didn't know it, but if you are a spiritual
seeker or are very loosely connected to the Christian
church, I was trying to evangelize you. If in the process I
offended you with something in this book, I apologize.
Trying to evangelize people with a book other than the
Bible is not the best. Why? Christianity is about relationship. You know me a little bit through this book, but I do
not know you. Relationships with people — and even God
— are a back-and-forth kind of thing.

My only goal for you with this book was to inspire
you to keep seeking God. If you would like to keep seeking by developing relationships with other seekers, then
go to www.wheresphilip.com and check out some studies
that you can complete online with someone.

To those already doing evangelism:

I am not sure the words I am about to share with you really exist. I read that they did, but I have not had a chance to check them out for myself. If you get the opportunity to visit London, or if you live there, you could perhaps check it out for me. The words I am talking about were supposedly engraved on a tomb in the crypts of Westminster Abbey — words written by an Anglican priest dating back 900 years ago:

When I was young and free and my imaginations had no limits, I dreamed of changing the world. As I grew older and wiser, I discovered the world would not change, so I shortened my sights somewhat and decided to change only my country.

But it, too, seemed immovable.

As I grew into my twilight years, in one last desperate attempt, I settled for changing only my family, those closest to me, but alas, they would have none of it.

And now as I lie on my deathbed, I suddenly realize: If I had only changed myself first, then by example I would have changed my family.

From their inspiration and encouragement, I would then have been able to better my country and, who knows, I may have even changed the world.

Everyone wants to go out somewhere and do evangelism — the farther, the more exotic, the more remote from one's own culture the better. But isn't it arrogant to think we can swoop into a culture we do not know for a week or two and think we have transformed other people with one program or another? Christianity is a relationship-based faith. Relationships take time. If you want to dedicate your whole life to another culture, perhaps then you will have a relationship base for leading others into a relationship with Christ.

The priest learned, too late, that there was nothing in his life that drew those around him toward God. He was eager to share, but had neglected to develop anything in his own life that was worth sharing. Too often, those of us engaged in evangelism do so with very little in our own lives to share. But evangelism starts with one's own relationship with God. It begins with a relationship worth sharing.

Often we travel far to evangelize because we want to give our boring faith a jolt of excitement. We want to get our teens enthusiastic about their faith. My question is: Why isn't the Christian faith exciting in our own homes? What about starting with ourselves and our families?

To those who have never done evangelism:

If you have never participated in evangelism before, maybe you shouldn't do it. If you have nothing to share, then you have nothing to share. Maybe that's why you've never done it. On the other hand, why not get something to share?

How? At the very least, start a relationship-based walk with God. Choose a daily Bible-reading goal and a prayer guide if needed. Do it every day. Enlist the help of your spouse if you are married. And why not your family? Perhaps some close friends. Maybe the whole church. You cannot have a walk with God without having a walk with God's family.

Next, look at your life and try to figure out what is keeping you from a fulfilling life with God and others. Are you too controlling? Are you too private? Are you too critical? What sin, what character flaw, is keeping God and people distant from you? These issues are relationship walls. God can help you over them. Often, He uses other people — people who have the same problem — to help. So pick a wall, and then find a Christian friend who struggles with the same wall and ask him or her to help you.

By God's grace, good things will start happening in your life and you will finally have something you can share with others. In fact, you will be eager to do it. Evangelism is not a technique. It is not a prepackaged formula. It is sharing the good news — the good news that you have experienced.

To pastors and church leaders who seek to lead others in evangelism:

Getting the people of your church to stop complaining about issues inside the church and to start sharing their faith with those outside the church is often quite a challenge. There are essentially two options: Build fishing pools, or teach your people how to fish.

Building fishing pools is the most popular choice — creating programs, craft fairs, sporting events, concerts, vacation Bible schools, seeker-sensitive services — any activity designed to gather many people in one place so that you can hopefully fish a few people out. It is a popular option, because it is relatively easy to get church people to build fishing pools. But here is the problem: In the end, somebody still has to know how to fish. Often, so much energy and expense go into building and maintaining the fishing pools that no one ever gets around to fishing. This book is ultimately recommending that you teach people how to fish.

There are are two keys to doing this: One is to fish, yourself. You cannot motivate people to do what you are not doing. And when you fish (do evangelism), make sure what you do is reproducible by everyone in your church. If your evangelism is some technique or program, then only those people with particular gifts will be able to do it. But if your evangelism comes out of your own walk with God and what that walk has done to change your life, well, everyone can do that.

The second key is to realize that evangelism will not take hold in your church until it becomes a culture — a way of life. Culture happens only when enough people are doing it. As a pastor, this is your job. You are in charge of the culture of your church. If you are a leader, then you must lead in the creation of a new culture. It will be hard. It will take time. But that is why you are there.

———

If you'd like help creating a culture of evangelism in your church or denomination, contact selzinga@bibleleague.org for information on seminars or consultations.

THE FINAL WORD

This book was not written just to get you excited about evangelism. It was written to introduce you to a new paradigm, a new perspective that says the habits in your personal life, your marriage, and your family will have the greatest effect on your ministry. It says that we teach what we know, but we reproduce what we are.

This new way of thinking starts with small things before big ones, gets you to see the church from the bottom up not the top down, advocates using the average many before the talented few, believes in walking with God before talking about Him. This paradigm says the key to great ministry is creating a church-wide culture of walking with God.

Each book in this series offers more ideas about how to create such a culture. Even if you're not specifically working on all five church ministries at once, read the whole series to get a good sense of what that culture looks like. Get your friends and your church leaders to read the books, too. Talk about them. Argue. Engage. Share. Pray. Make changes in your life. God will help.

www. StevenElzinga.com
Music • Preaching • Evangelism
Discipleship • Leadership

ABOUT THE AUTHOR

Steven Elzinga serves as the Director of the Bible League's USA ministry and as the pastor of a church in Michigan. This dual role allows him to assist many churches without losing touch with life on the front lines.

His overwhelming passion is to see ordinary Christians do something — play an instrument, read through the entire Bible, share a walk with God with someone — that they thought they could never do. He is excited to watch people cast off supposed limitations and open themselves to the possibilities God has for them.

Steven lives in the Grand Rapids area with his wife and four sons.

ORDERING INFORMATION

The ideas in this book are meant to be shared with other people. Accordingly, we've made this book as inexpensive as possible so you can afford to buy one for anyone you think might find it interesting — those involved in evangelism, those who've never tried evangelism, those wondering what Christianity is all about. You may purchase this book in lots of 10 for $2.99 (USD) apiece. Individual copies are only $3.99.

In the United States you may order online by visiting our website at http://www.StevenElzinga.com/evangelism.

To order by mail or phone, use the following contact information for your country:

UNITED STATES:
1-800-871-5445
Bible League
PO Box 28000
Chicago, IL 60628

AUSTRALIA:
1-800-800-937
The Bible League
PO Box 4071
Werrington NSW 2747

CANADA:
1-800-363-9673
The Bible League
PO Box 5037
Burlington ON, L7R 3Y8

NEW ZEALAND:
+ 9-846-5111
Bible League
PO Box 77-047
Mt Albert, Auckland 1030